decorating

the *smart* approach to design

CREATIVE HOMEOWNER®

decorating

the *smart* approach to design

CREATIVE HOMEOWNER®, Upper Saddle River, New Jersey

DECORATING: THE SMART APPROACH TO DESIGN

SENIOR EDITOR	Kathie Robitz
GRAPHIC DESIGNER	Kathryn Wityk
PROOFREADER	Sara M. Markowitz
DIGITAL IMAGING SPECIALIST	Mary Dolan
INDEXER	Erica Caridio, The Last Word
INTERIOR DESIGN CONCEPT	Glee Barre, David Geer
COVER DESIGN CONCEPT	Glee Barre
FRONT COVER PHOTOGRAPHY	Eric Roth
BACK COVER PHOTOGRAPHY	*top* Mark Lohman; *bottom* Bob Greenspan, stylist: Susan Andrews

CREATIVE HOMEOWNER

VICE PRESIDENT AND PUBLISHER	Timothy O. Bakke
MANAGING EDITOR	Fran J. Donegan
ART DIRECTOR	David Geer
PRODUCTION COORDINATOR	Sara M. Markowitz

Current Printing (last digit)
10 9 8 7 6 5 4 3 2 1

Manufactured in the United States of America

Decorating: The Smart Approach to Design
Library of Congress Control Number: 2011921414
ISBN-10: 1-58011-529-2
ISBN-13: 978-1-58011-529-2

CREATIVE HOMEOWNER®
A Division of Federal Marketing Corp.
24 Park Way
Upper Saddle River, NJ 07458
www.creativehomeowner.com

acknowledgments

For their expertise, thank you goes to the following
designers: Lynn LoCascio, Allied Member, ASID; Molly McLean;
Lyn Peterson; Lucianna Samu; Darryl Tucker, ASID, CID;
Amy Wax; and Barbara Winfield

contents

introduction

Creating a home that is comfortable, personal, and in sync with your life-style is doable on almost any budget when you give careful consideration to a few things. For success, you'll want to learn the key concepts professional designers use to pull together beautiful interiors. You'll find the guidance and inspiration you need for everything from tips for arranging furniture to choosing a color scheme right here in *Decorating: The Smart Approach to Design*. Let's get started...

The easy elegance of this room is the result of patience and planning.

chapter 1

design 101

- ◆ **THINK LIKE A DESIGNER**
- ◆ **SCALE AND PROPORTION**
- ◆ **LINE**
- ◆ **BALANCE**
- ◆ **HARMONY AND RHYTHM**
- ◆ **IT'S IN THE DETAILS**

Knowing a few tricks of the trade can help you decorate your home with the finesse that you've admired about professionally designed interiors. The basic concepts of design are easy to understand and apply with a little practice. This chapter introduces you to these simple ideas and shows you how to look at space and objects in an entirely new way. Keep these concepts in mind when you're shopping for furnishings and fabrics, too. Are you ready? Get started!

Learning the basic concepts of scale, proportion, line, balance, rhythm, and harmony will make you a decorating star!

Think Like a Designer

Most people decorate their homes simply with what they like, helped in some cases by a little native know-how. But if you want the pulled-together look that professionals and the lucky few with an "eye" for such things are able to achieve with ease, start to think like a designer.

Although there are no strict rules to follow, serious students of design approach each project mindful of these fundamental concepts: scale, proportion, line, balance, harmony, and rhythm. Use these simple concepts to create a cohesive interior that is appealing to the eye. Their application can also help you resolve some of the vexing issues of dealing with awkwardly configured physical space.

The following pages will explain each of the concepts and how to use them to your advantage.

In a small room, opposite, balancing pattern with physical space is important. In order to adjust the overall scale of this sunroom, above, and make it more cozy, the designer covered the top portion of the windows with solid shades that visually lower the height of the ceiling.

Scale and Proportion

Scale simply refers to the size of something as it relates to the size of everything else, including people and the physical space. **Proportion** refers to the relationship of parts or objects to one another based on size—the size of the window is in proportion to the size of the room, for example. Good scale is achieved when all of the parts are proportionately correct relative to each other, as well as to the whole.

Although it is easy to see that something is too large or too small for its place, it takes a deliberate effort to achieve good proportion. It requires patience and sometimes experimentation with objects or arrangements until you get it right.

It's all relative. The deep paint color on the upper portion of the walls, opposite, visually tones down the height of the room so that the furnishings appear in proportion to the size of the space. In another example, the visual scale of this frame, above, is affected by its proportional relationship to the chair.

get smart

BE PREPARED

Keep a measuring tape in the glove compartment of your car or a small one in your purse. If you come across something that you think would look perfect in your home, you'll be able to confirm whether it's the right size for the space.

We bought a house with a barn-size room addition and a vaulted ceiling. How can I make the space feel less cavernous?

what the experts say

A lot depends on your furniture. Asheboro, North Carolina, interior designer Molly McLean says, "The best rule of thumb is to figure out what your largest piece [of furniture] or focal point is going to be. For example, if it is a living or family room, your sofa and chairs are the main point. In a bedroom, the bed is the center attraction. A good way to look at it is like this: the main piece or grouping can take up about 40 percent of the room, leaving about 10 to 15 percent for other pieces and 40 percent for walking space. Although the ceiling may be high, you have to take into account the actual floor space.

"A higher ceiling will need a taller headboard or a larger piece above your existing headboard to draw the eye upward in a bedroom, for example.

"Window treatments can also make a large room feel less imposing; adding throw pillows and accessories helps, too, as does arrangements or groupings of artwork on large walls."

Light fixtures are another way to visually tone down the scale of a room with a high ceiling. The right pendant or chandelier, however, must be properly installed and scaled in proportion to the space. If it's too small or hangs too high, it will look wrong. See chapter 7, "Let There Be Lighting," beginning on page 180, for installation tips.

This framed print is the size of some furniture pieces, solving the problem of a blank wall and limited floor space.

Line

Simply put, **line** defines space. Two-dimensional space consists of flat surfaces, such as walls, floors, and ceilings, which are formed by intersecting lines. Adding depth, or volume, to a flat surface creates three-dimensional space such as a room. However, lines also suggest various qualities.

Vertical lines imply strength, dignity, and formality—a classical column, for example, which always appears stately, strong, and masculine. **Horizontal lines,** such as the lines of a bed or a sturdy platform, on the other hand, convey relaxation and security. **Diagonal lines,** such as those of a balustrade or a gable, express motion, transition, and change. **Curved lines** have a feminine quality and denote freedom, softness, and sensuality.

Look at the lines suggested by the architecture in your space, and add interest by introducing something new or in contrast to what already exists.

Stripes, especially vertical ones, are a visually strong motif for fabrics and other textiles. On curtain panels and upholstery, they are well suited to this traditional-style home.

do this... not that

get it straight

Stripes can add a lot of personality to a room, whether you paint them on a wall or use fabrics with a stripe pattern.

Vertical stripes are considered more traditional. If your tastes lean toward Modern design, use horizontal stripes. And if you're just using stripes on your throw pillows, arrange them any way the mood strikes you.

This homeowner chose a striped fabric that picks up the pumpkin color of the chair. Blue, orange's complement, is a standout accent color.

This staircase is an excellent visual example of what is suggested by diagonal lines—motion or transition. Playful fabrics and colors are a pleasing counterpoint to the formal lines of the architecture.

An asymmetrical arrangement of objects on this cart, above, has a more casual,
contemporary look as compared with the symmetrical placement of the windows, opposite.

Balance

Balance refers to the equilibrium among forms in a room. With balance, relationships between objects seem natural and comfortable to the eye. For instance, two framed pictures of relatively equal size and weight look appropriate hanging side by side on a wall, whereas the pairing of two pictures of unequal size and weight seems awkward and out of balance. Balanced relationships can be symmetrical or asymmetrical.

Symmetry refers to the exact same arrangement of parts, objects, or forms on both sides of an imagined or real center line. It is formal and typical of traditional styles of architecture and design.

Asymmetry refers to the balance between objects of different sizes as the result of placement. As long as the scale is correct, asymmetry can be every bit as pleasing as symmetry. Asymmetrical arrangements are informal, as is most contemporary design.

Harmony and Rhythm

Two other concepts, harmony and rhythm, concern creating patterns in space. **Harmony** is achieved in design when all of the elements relate to one another. In other words, everything coordinates within one scheme or motif. Matching or compatible styles, colors, and patterns, are good examples. **Rhythm** refers to repetition—in patterns, motifs, colors, and so forth. You'll read more about these two concepts and their application in Chapter 4, "Color, Pattern, and Texture," beginning on page 50.

For now, keep in mind that harmony pulls a room together, while rhythm connects the dots, so to speak, keeping your eye and interest going to different areas of the room. The key to creating good rythm and harmony is balance—and always add a contrasting element to liven up the look.

Color is the outstanding element that unites an eclectic collection of furnishings, below, resulting in a cohesive design.

The lively print in the curtain panels, above, picks up on the tangerine theme and adds excitement to the design.

Pillows, left, scattered throughout carry the tangerine-inspired theme around the room. A grouping of small prints keeps the eye moving.

This take on Scandinavian style is young and inviting. **Far right:** Vintage traditional furniture pieces are arranged symmetrically against the main wall. The bed is dressed in a cheerful check and florals, which are repeated around the room, offsetting the formal appearance of the antique pieces.

The chair-rail molding that horizontally divides the wall in half helps to create the sense of restfulness that is reinforced

it's in the
details ✳

by the room's wall color.

Top right: A painted floral swag near the top of the wall alludes to a traditional Swedish motif.

Bottom right: A quiet nook, dressed in coordinating fabrics, overlooks the garden.

find out more

@ www.nordicstyle.com
www.laylagrace.com

chapter 2
making space

Your house has its own set of bones and, unless you're making structural changes, you've got to work with them. But there are a number of ways to use or visually shape a space to make it work for you. Before you make any decisions about furnishing the rooms in your home, get to know the space. If you plan ahead, even challenging spaces—those that are too small, oddly configured, or even too large—will come together gracefully.

Almost any space can be functional and fabulous when you emphasize its good points, such as handsome architectural treatments, and down-play less-attractive features.

Space Planning

You need the rooms in your home to be functional and aesthetically pleasing. In many cases, that can be a challenge but not impossible to achieve with planning. Begin by making notes about what you think are the best and worst features of the space.

Look at the layout in terms of permanent features, such as doors and doorways, windows, stairs, and closets. Are any shapes awkward? Consider adjacent spaces, too. Do they present problems concerning noise or privacy? Note the orientation of the windows at various times of the day. Is there a view?

Jot down all of the activities you expect the space to accommodate and whether your budget allows for any structural alterations. Now you're ready to analyze the existing physical space.

Grouping seating pieces near the fireplace creates a cozy atmosphere for conversation, right and opposite. The large mirror is a decorating device for amplifying a sense of space.

Lighten up! Modest-size rooms can look and feel more spacious if you keep to light colors and edit furniture pieces, sticking with what's necessary and suitable for the size of the space. Simply using a table and chairs in this dining area, left, suffices and leaves lots of room for guests to mingle when the party's on!

smart steps Put It on Paper

STEP 1 measure up

Invest in a good steel measuring tape, and take careful, accurate dimensions of the space. If you can, ask another family member or a friend to help; he or she can hold the end of the tape in one corner while you measure the entire length of a wall in a single step. This eliminates the possibility of the cumulative error that often occurs when measuring a wall in increments.

If a window or doorway breaks up the space, measure from one corner of the wall to the outer edge of the opening, and then proceed from the outer edge to the next corner.

STEP 2 draw a floor plan

Make a free-hand sketch of the space and its permanent features, such as doors and windows, noting all dimensions on the plan or in the margin. Pencil in electrical switches and outlets, cable input jacks, phone jacks, radiators, heat registers, air ducts, and light fixtures as well. Indicate adjoining rooms or areas on the sketch, too. You don't want to block access to any of them.

For accuracy, you may want to redraw the layout to scale on ¼-inch graph paper. Make each square represent one foot. This will be helpful when it's time to choose and arrange furniture.

Making the Most of It

et's face it: unless you can afford to make expensive structural alterations, you'll have to make the most of what you've got. Often, that means being smart about how you furnish the room. This is when your floor plan comes in handy.

If the shape of the space bothers you, there are simple tricks that play on the eye to camouflage the problem visually. For example, if the room is **long,** divide it into two separate groupings of furniture.

Use area rugs to anchor each group. You can also use square shapes, such as a square area rug, to "widen" the space. If the room is **narrow,** arrange furniture on the diagonal and introduce more squares—tables, rugs, or ottomans, for example. For a room with a **low** ceiling, add height with tall furnishings—chests, bookcases, tall lamps, or curtains that extend above the window frame to the floor. Use vertical lines, even on wall and fabric treatments.

In these tight quarters, a chair and ottoman placed diagonally in a corner leave enough clearance to move around the bed to the bathroom.

do this... not that

tea for two ... or three!

In a small kitchen, don't sacrifice important floor space in the work area by cramming in a table and chairs. Instead, check out this solution, right, which makes use of a small corner. The bench is a great idea for seating more than one, and the round table takes up a minimum amount of space.

Dormer windows do not have to limit functional space. Build closets into the eaves, and make use of the area below the window with built-in furnishings. Here, a simple shelf becomes a desk.

Go with the flow. In many cases, the secret to arranging furniture effectively in a space is not to push it up against the walls. **Far right:** In this comfortable living room, an area rug anchors the seating area, which is arranged to view both the fireplace and the TV.

Top right: Visually linked to this room by color and a wood floor that flows throughout the dining area, the space basks in natural light. **Bottom right:** To reflect more of that space-expanding

it's in the details ✳

natural light, there is a mirrored sideboard cabinet against the wall.

find area rugs
@ www.karastan.com
www.homedecorators.com

Furniture Arrangements

The placement of each piece of furniture depends on the room's shape. Long, narrow spaces work better when divided into distinct areas for different functions. Square rooms offer the option of grouping furniture in the middle of the room. Think about how you use the room; this will help you with deciding on a layout or floor plan.

Furniture can be used to efficiently divide space. Within a large room, you could create a cozy sitting area in front of a fireplace and position an entertainment center in another area. Or if you need to define separate living and dining areas within one space, a sofa with a low back can act as a divider, as can an étagère, a decorative screen, or a long table. Modular seating pieces are practical if you need your layout to be flexible.

P.S.: If you are having trouble creating a pleasing arrangement of furniture in a room, it can help to remove all of the contents and start from scratch.

It's smart to include a few seating pieces in your plan that can be rearranged easily. Ottomans and chairs on casters can go against the walls or out of the room when they are not needed.

Q&A

What are some suggestions for making the most of space in a modest-size room that is used as a TV room?

what the experts say

"First, decide on the location of the TV," recommends interior designer Barbara Winfield. "It's important that the screen be easily viewed from any angle in the room but positioned so that daylight glare won't interfere with viewing. Today's large flat-screen TVs have a tendency to overwhelm a modest-size room. You can visually minimize its impact by placing the TV in a large wall unit, one that is designed to accommodate storage for media equipment, stereos, and CDs and DVDs."

(Your optimal viewing comfort depends on the distance you place between you and the screen. To determine what's best for you, use a viewing distance calculator, which you can find on a number of Web sites.)

"Upholstery should be casual and comfortable," adds Winfield. "I would suggest a loveseat or small sofa and two apartment-size recliners. Choose double-duty furniture: storage ottomans that can be used for seating, coffee tables with shelves, and end tables with pull-out shelves to hold beverages and drawers to hold remote controls and DVD storage.

"For window treatments, select a combination of adjustable blinds to let in light combined with room-darkening draperies. Because the room is a modest size, I would choose fabrics in a light color to offset the heaviness of the draperies."

Built-in cabinets can store a lot of things and keep other items off the floor.

Focal Points

Sometimes a room has a special feature, a focal point or centerpiece where the eye can rest. A focal point may be either built into the architecture or brought in as part of the decor. In a large room, there may be more than one focal point.

Architecturally speaking, a fireplace is usually a focal point. A large window or tall built-in bookcases are two more examples. So obviously, scale has something to do with it. Keep that in mind if your room needs a focal point.

If your room lacks an architectural focal point, create a feature wall—paint one large surface a bold or contrasting color. Fill a wall with a collection displayed on shelves or with art. Bring in a massive piece of furniture, such as an armoire or tall chest if the room can handle it. Do something dramatic with the window treatments. Make a statement.

Composed of attractive objects, this vignette, opposite, is a secondary focal point in a room. The fireplace, above—an important architectural feature—commands attention, as does a large piece of furniture, such as the armoire below.

Sight Lines

When you're decorating a room, keep the adjacent spaces in mind. Although this is especially important in an open plan, it applies to any type of interior—even those with rooms that are almost entirely closed off from one another.

Remember the design concept of harmony? Here is where it begs to be applied. Perhaps it's not important that the rooms in your home flow seamlessly from one to the other. But at the very least, be sensitive to what you will see from every point around the room, trying to make sure that the combination doesn't offend the eye.

One way to address sight lines is with color—either a coordinated palette throughout the house or one of exciting contrasts. Another way is by arranging objects, such as furniture, in a way that directs your eye toward something pleasant or interesting.

do this... not that

the vantage point

A perfect example of sight-line sensitivity is this view into the powder room, below. Despite space limitations and the location of plumbing lines, the designer kept the toilet out of sight.

Whether you're looking outdoors, left, or into an adjacent room, above, be mindful of sight lines when you're arranging space.

1 fireplace

3 wall decor

the top **10**

Ideas for Focal Points

1 fireplaces This is a no brainer. The size of some fireplaces demands that you stop and take notice. If your fireplace is nondescript, boost its appeal by refacing it in stone, replacing the mantel, adding decorative trimwork to the overmantel or the face, creating a vignette on the mantel, or adding a handsome fire screen.

2 architectural windows Large, dramatic windows, often called "architectural windows," can be showstoppers in any room in the house. If you are lucky enough to have even one, you may want to leave it uncovered, revealing its architectural lines—unless your house is too close to the neighbors or the view is subpar.

5 the TV

3 wall decor One picture or a grouping of framed prints, paintings, or photographs not only calls attention to itself but adds personality to your room's decor. An alternative to framed art is a tapestry, a large vintage quilt, or some other display-worthy textile. Additional ideas include mirrors, wall clocks, objets d'art displayed on brackets, plates, and maps.

4 a feature wall The main wall in a room painted a color that contrasts with the other walls or an intensely saturated shade becomes a focal point. An alternative is a patterned wallpaper, a mural, or a trompe l'oeil painted wall.

5 the TV The TV is typically a focal point in a family or TV room, particularly if the screen is prominent.

6 large furniture pieces Anchor a room or a section of a large space with a substantial piece of furniture.

7 window treatments Some window treatments command attention, particularly formal styles or ones with patterned fabrics.

8 built-ins Large built-in furnishings, such as media cabinets, bookcases, and window seats, can be focal points.

9 chandeliers and some light fixtures A dramatic chandelier or hanging fixture is often a room's main attraction.

10 a grand staircase In an entry hall, a grand staircase provides the wow factor.

do this... not that

cut the line

This long and narrow kitchen looks a lot homier thanks to the short but effective peninsula that breaks up the space without obstructing it. Banks of tall cabinets offer extra storage but could overwhelm another space that didn't have this warm wood paneling on the ceiling to add a cozy ambiance.

A clever way to visually widen a room is to set furniture or, as in this case, a rug on the diagonal. Using a round coffee table helps to break up the boxiness of the space.

Visual Tricks

t's probably safe to say that most people live with space that isn't perfect. But it doesn't necessarily require complicated or expensive structural changes to make some less-than-perfect rooms look and feel a lot less awkward or ill proportioned.

Remember the discussion about line? (See page 18 in Chapter 1.) You can play with line to make the shape of a room more pleasing to the eye. It's a trick that professionals use all the time and one that you can easily make work for you. Are your ceilings low? Hang curtains high above the window frame to give the illusion of a taller room.

Color—once again—comes to the rescue. This is another nifty tool for shaping and reshaping space visually. (For more about this, see Chapter 3, "Color," beginning on page 50.) Using light and cool colors opens up a space; it's a useful device when a room is small. Deep and warm colors have the opposite effect on space. When a room feels too large or too tall, as is often the case in open-plan layouts with double-height ceilings, applying a warm color to the walls can make the space feel less imposing and more cozy.

Vaulted ceilings can be dramatic but cold. That's why these homeowners were smart to choose deeply saturated and warm paint colors to tone down the scale of the space.

This somewhat modest-size city apartment appears larger than it really is, thanks to a few tricks. **Far right:** The main living area has to accommodate several functions and all of the furniture that goes with them, including upholstered seating, a dining table, bookcases, and a desk. So what's the trick? Mirrors, which visually expand the room. **Top right:** Furniture that is the proper scale for the space helps too, along

it's in the
details *

with an all-white palette. **Bottom right:** A small folding screen unobtrusively creates a separate space for the office.

find mirrors

@ www.restorationhardware.com
   www.ballarddesigns.com

making space

chapter 3
color

Color is a very personal choice. Despite fads and trends, your own preferences should be your guide when you are deciding on a color scheme for your home. Some designers suggest maintaining a color link from room to room, especially in an open layout—using different shades, tints, and prints of the same color for variety. But you don't have to lock yourself into just a couple of basic colors. Express your love of color your way.

This fresh green palette and lively floral print create a happy carefree feeling.

A golden yellow, accented with autumnal brown, russet, and pumpkin, is warm and welcoming in this home's front hall.

An Artful Science

Color is the most versatile tool a designer or homeowner can use. It is both the easiest way to update an interior and an effective tool to visually alter it. It is the most exciting decorating element, changing a room with ease.

For some reason, many people find the power of color intimidating and, fearful of stepping into new territory, stick with neutrals. So the palette for walls is often neutral—colors that work fine as a backdrop for more richly hued furnishings. However, they are less successful in rooms with neutral-colored furnishings because, believe it or not, there are so many variations of them that it's sometimes hard to make a match.

Aside from the strength of color itself, the enormity of color choices in everything from paint to furniture and flooring can be overwhelming, causing a retreat to the safety of white or beige. So how do you break the monotony and establish an exciting scheme? Trial and error is one way. If that's too risky, you can't go wrong consulting "Color Wheel Basics." (See page 54.)

Soft peach walls and crisp white trim form a perfect subtle backdrop for this room's large tangerine-orange sofa.

Color Wheel Basics

The color wheel is a fixed, circular arrangement of colors that reveals their relationship to one another. Start with the **primaries**—red, yellow, and blue. All other colors are made from these three. Mixing red and yellow, for example, produces a **secondary** color, in this case, orange. Mixing together one secondary and one primary color, such as blue and green, will produce a blue-green, which is a **tertiary** color. Turquoise is an example. There are six tertiary colors. In addition to blue-green, there is yellow-orange, red-orange, red-violet, blue-violet, and yellow-green.

Colors such as yellow-green and red-violet oppose one another on the color wheel, so they are **complementary.** Colors that are adjacent on the color wheel—blue and green, for example—are called **"analogous."** A good rule of thumb for an attractive analogous scheme is to use no more than two primary colors.

A **split-complementary** scheme contains three colors—one complementary and two analogous. Varying the value of the colors can produce either soft or dramatic results.

Finally, a **monochromatic** scheme is based entirely on various tints and shades of a single color. Monochromatic neutral schemes with shades and tones of beige, gray, brown, black, and white could be described otherwise, technically. But this collection is generally accepted as a monochromatic neutral palette.

As you play with the color wheel, you'll come to feel more comfortable creating a color scheme.

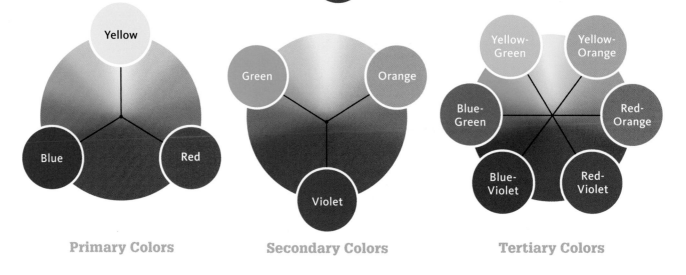

Primary Colors

Yellow
Blue
Red

Secondary Colors

Green
Orange
Violet

Tertiary Colors

Yellow-Green
Yellow-Orange
Blue-Green
Red-Orange
Blue-Violet
Red-Violet

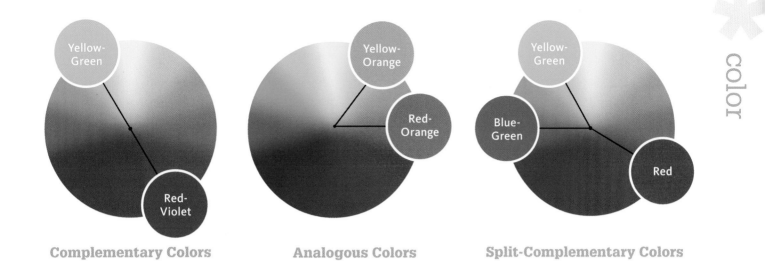

Complementary Colors

Analogous Colors

Split-Complementary Colors

This homeowner isn't shy about using color, and the multicolor scheme of warm hues she selected is inviting.

Primarily Red

Warm colors such as red and yellow energize a room and seem to advance, making a space feel cozy or pushing an element into the foreground. Red is festive and lively. When it's undiluted, this engaging color is particularly effective in rooms where people socialize. It seems to put everyone in a convivial mood and stimulates conversation. Not to mention everyone looks better in its rosy glow. How-

ever, you have to be careful when using a saturated red. Although red will look spectacular, it will also soak up the light because it has no reflective value.

In a small space, play it safe, using red on a feature wall instead of painting the entire room. Or try using a few red accessories. If you still want to paint a small room red, use a high-performance enamel, which has a sheen.

Red is a terrific choice for this dining room, below, where the owners entertain frequently. The energetic red on this pool table, right, enhances the lively mood for playing games.

Pink

Think pink—and not just for little girls' rooms. This lightened version of red, in fact, has many moods that can range from wistful pastel tints to "shocking" hot pinks and corals. Pink is actually quite versatile and lets you add a hint of red's warmth without its assertiveness.

If you think pink is too feminine, try pairing it with gray, a combination that can be surprisingly sophisticated. The more gray elements, the more tailored and masculine the effect.

Pink is also enhanced by complementary green, and the effect of a juxaposition with cool blue may make pink warmer and stronger by contrast. Teamed with yellow or neutrals, pink's warmth is intensified even more, especially that of the coral pinks.

Pinks and reds, with hints of green and blue, look charming in this dining room, opposite. Timid about using pink? Try it as an accent or with accessories, such as this hot pink pillow, right.

Orange

Earthy and vivacious, orange is not a color for the fainthearted. The range of this warm color's tones goes from blazing bright hues to soft melon and peach tints to deep autumnal and rugged terra-cotta shades.

Pure, saturated orange is high-energy, eye-catching color. Like red, it's a bold, advancing hue that can be used successfully as an accent in playrooms or in rooms meant for short stays where high drama is on the menu. Again like red, it's also a convival color, stimulating the appetite and conversation of dinner guests.

Orange's softer side is flattering to most skin tones, and deepened terra-cotta shades lend a warm, comfortable feeling to a room.

Accents in greens and blues offer cooling contrasts to orange, which always pairs well with earth tones.

get smart
EASY DOES IT

Even when it's your favorite color, orange is intense. Try using it in layers, building from soft to saturated. Paint the walls a pale tint of orange, reserving more vivid versions of the hue for soft furnishings, such as curtains, upholstery, and accents.

The orange walls in this room, oppsite and above, are high octane as they bask in the light of day. But at night, this warm color feels cozy and warm. It's no accident that the wall color, also found in the rug, picks up the wood tones in the floor and furniture.

Primarily Yellow

Cheerful yellow can warm even the chilliest of rooms. A very pale tint can be a warmer alternative to white, providing an appealing but shy luminescence as a background color. It can enhance sunlight or create the illusion of more sun where there is actually little natural light. However, you must be careful when choosing yellow for a wall color. Strong tints can be overpowering in a room that gets intense afternoon or all-day sun.

Because of yellow's interaction with light, textures

are particularly important. Bright or pastel yellows seem airy in silks and damasks, while soft, earthier shades are cozier in velvet or woolen weaves.

Yellow's direct complement is violet, but it finds a sense of balance with blue. Lemon yellow contrasts richly with warm red-tinged blues, while deep yellow becomes golden paired with rich reds and deep blues.

This yellow-upholstered chair, opposite, pops out against an all-white room. A spring garden inspired this family room's cheerful palette, below, which uses yellow as the main color, with green and blue serving as accents.

Green

A mixture of yellow and blue, green's balance of warm and cool is easy on the eyes, with a space-enhancing tendency to recede. Although green is technically a secondary hue, many people regard it as a "psychological primary" that is basic.

Nature showcases the many shades and tints of green, mixing them freely. But be careful, certain blue-greens and yellow-greens may fight if you use them equally.

Deep shades play off white and cream handsomely. Acid greens are bold and modern. Blue-greens can look more blue or more green, depending on the light. Grayed greens, such as soft sage and moss, are often used as neutrals.

Green is a color that goes anywhere. It works well with red, its complement, and with many shades of violet.

Green adds a dramatic burst of color to both of these rooms, right and opposite. Bright white painted woodwork and crisp white slipcovers on some of the furniture accentuate the freshness of the color.

do this... not that

eliminate the guesswork

When you're thinking about painting walls green, don't just choose a shade from a paint chip. Green can be tricky, and getting the shade just right can take a little extra effort.

There are many variations of green. Are you aiming for a cool minty hue, which has more blue in it, or a pale olive, which has more yellow in it? Buy a small amount, and try the color on the walls. Actually, this is what you should do with any color.

If a particular green object is what inspires you, take it with you to the paint store where they can match it.

Pale peach-colored walls are beautifully complemented by blue, especially rich warm variations of the color. The painting over the fireplace illustrates the colors that result from the blending of blue and green.

Primarily Blue

B lue is a color with endless moods—sleek navy, summery azure, vivid cobalt, delicate robin's egg, or blazing lapis—to name a few.

With the exception of some blue tints with red undertones, blue is the essence of cool. It can temper a glaringly sunny room, although the same decor might feel icy in a space lacking in natural light.

The color remains true across its many tints and shades, however, and they all mix well together. But blue's strong personality gains something from the right contrast. White, for example, is a clean foil, and yellow works well with blue of equal intensity whether it's a pastel or saturated version of the colors. Its complement, orange, plays a better supporting role in an interior when it's a softened peach or a deep amber.

Blue and green have an inherent harmony. Between these two hues on the color wheel, you'll find beautifully ambiguous blends—teal, turquoise, and aqua—that often look best when they are paired with warm accents.

Because blue is regarded as a restful color, it's a popular choice for bedrooms. Here, the white-painted furniture keeps the color from becoming overdone.

Violet

Once reserved for royalty, violet (or purple) is a secondary color that is created by mixing red and blue. It is a highly saturated hue that requires precision when you paint with it; be sure you have enough for the job before you begin. Technology aside, super-saturated colors never mix the same way twice.

A shade containing lots of red, such as magenta, can be lively and warm; strengthening its blue component results in a cool hue, such as lavender. Eggplant and plum are the most dramatic shades, deepened by adding black. They are also very subjective—you either love them or hate them.

You can harmoniously pair violet with either of its two components, red or blue. Light-green and lavender or lilac is always a pretty combination. In fact, the pale gray- and blue-like versions are quite lovely.

If you're willing to take a chance on it, this color can give a boost to any dull palette.

Lavender with turquoise—and a dab or two of pink and yellow—is a charming look for this girl's room, above and below. Cream-color shades and carpeting keeps the palette calm. A super-saturated eggplant is a gutsy color choice that paid off handsomely in this dining room, opposite.

Neutrals

Technically, true neutrals are black and white, but for decorating, the category also extends to off-whites and creams, beiges, and browns, as well as the natural textures of wood, stone, grasses (such as bamboo), and metals.

Easy-going, mixable neutrals and naturals often play a supporting role in design, but they are capable of carrying the whole show. Light neutrals enhance a sense of space and provide an unobtrusive backdrop for more dramatic colors in accessories. Darker neutrals

are forgiving of daily wear. But beyond their usefulness, neutrals can be charming and relaxing.

All-white rooms can be impressive. But remember that white comes in all sorts of shades and tones. Be sure to compare each varying shade. Those with green or blue undertones will be cool, while red and yellow undertones will produce warmer whites.

This handsome stone fireplace, opposite, inspired a neutral palette for the room. All eyes are on the large red print, below, which stands out against a background of white walls.

Each of these white rooms features touches of black for an interesting contrast and some warming accents—a wood floor, above, a basket, opposite top, and a hint of earthier hues from an adjacent room, opposite bottom.

Black and White

Pure bright white can be dazzling and make companion colors more luminous. A colorless backdrop (white is actually the absence of color) emphasizes furniture and artwork.

Black adds drama and strong forms to a room. It has gradations from soft charcoal to darkest ebony, many with tints and undertones of red or blue. Matte textures make black more dense, while glossy finishes seem livelier.

A strictly all-black-and-white room can appear quite formal and somewhat sterile. The inherent warmth of wood or a touch of wicker can mellow the contrast, as can an accent or hint of color from an accessory.

Where do I begin to develop a color scheme that stands the test of time? Is it all about theory? I get tired of wall colors so quickly.

what the experts say

Finding your perfect palette is actually a highly personal process. "There are certain places in your imagination and memory that hold fast to colors you have associated with pleasure," says Lucianna Samu, an interior designer and color expert. "Therefore, recognizing an affinity for certain colors is a logical way to begin planning a palette.

"The means to a colorful home, then, is to tell your personal color story—and not necessarily on the walls, especially if you tire of colors easily. Look for exciting ways to express your preferences in fabric, art, and accessories. Just keep in mind that you may have to overcome some color prejudices to ground a palette—pairing gray with a vivid accent, for example, or using several shades of brown in a room with lots of blue.

"Remember, avoiding certain colors can leave your rooms feeling cold. Little touches of cool gray or acorn brown may be more enticing than you would have believed. And you may find that using buttery oranges, hot pinks, and persimmon with wild abandon is freeing after all."

Sometimes you can change the entire look or mood of a room by swapping just one of the room's main colors for another. See how different this room looks when the chair fabric changes from orange to teal.

Creating a Color Scheme

Everyone has a favorite color. But committing that color to an entire palette isn't always easy. The one thing you don't want to do is go with a color fad unless you use it only as an accent that can be easily changed when the trend passes. What we're talking about is choosing a wall color and furnishings that are harmonious together and enhance the physical space. If the room is cool, choose a color that you like from the warm hues on the wheel. Do the opposite if the room needs cooling down. Too much of one color will be boring unless you mix it up with different shades and tones.

If you're starting from scratch, remember that it's easier to have a paint color custom mixed to coordinate with your furnishings than to have to find upholstered pieces that go with the walls you've already painted. Put a small board together with samples of paint chips and fabrics, adding and removing items until you find a winning scheme.

Bold colors can be used successfully when relief is supplied by a neutral, such as white. Chocolate walls look scrumptious and cozy mixed with other earth tones, below. A Kelly green band is spectacular with soft blues and white, opposite.

Color, pattern, and texture come together pleasingly in this youthful bedroom.

Right: Pretty textiles in perky pink, green, and yellow in stripes, solids, and a chinoiserie print look lively yet soft. The natural woven blinds and headboard bring texture into the room.

Opposite top: Tone-on-tone shades of green make up the striped pattern in the curtain panels. A pink band was added along the edge to draw the eye and link to other pink details in the room.

it's in the details *

Opposite bottom: A chair painted yellow-green and paired with a pink-and-white-striped cushion picks up colors in the pillows.

find natural woven furniture
@ www.seagrass-furniture.com
www.crateandbarrel.com

This soft palette is as cool and breezy as the sea. **Far right:** Pale aqua-green walls reflect the sunlight beautifully in this space. The colors of the sea and sand in the oil painting became the inspiration for the room's color scheme. But the design is more sophisticated than that of a casual beach cottage.

Top right: Throw pillows and other accessories also pick up colors found in the painting and help to link the theme throughout.

it's in the details ✳

Bottom right: The dining room, which is open to the living area, continues the palette, adding a few warmer accent tones.

find color inspiration
@ www.myperfectcolor.com
www.pantone.com

* color

Perk It Up with Pattern

A room without pattern can be rather dull. But even if you're timid about using patterns and prints, you don't have to use a lot of them to liven up your scheme.

Large-scale patterns are like warm colors in that they appear to come toward you. They can create a lively mood and generally make a large space feel more cozy. In a small room, however, a large pattern can overpower the space; use it sparingly or where you don't spend a lot of time, such as in a powder room or a hallway.

Small patterns appear to recede, which means that in a large space or from a distance, they may read as a solid color, so choose one with a bright colorway. Small patterns can also effectively camouflage odd angles or corners, such as those in attic ceilings.

Wallpaper, opposite, is an easy way to add pattern to a bland room. In general, large prints work best in large spaces. Fabric is an obvious choice for using a print either on curtains, pillows, or upholstery, left. Don't forget flooring, above, as an opportunity to introduce pattern to a room.

Become a Mix Master

Afraid to mix patterns? Here's the trick: use the same scale, theme, or color to link the different prints. The regularity of checks, stripes, textural looks, and geometrics, particularly if they're small in scale and low in contrast, tends to make them easy-to-mix "neutral" patterns. A small floral can play off a thin ticking stripe, while a large floral chintz may require a bolder stripe as a same-scale foil. Use the same or similar patterns in varying sizes, or develop a theme by focusing on florals, geometrics, or ethnic prints.

The most effective link is shared colors or a similar level of intensity between the prints. A solid-color companion that pulls out a hue shared by two prints provides another connection. Experiment to see the combinations that work for you.

Color is the key that connects the mix of colors and motifs, left and below. The designer used large, medium, and small prints to create a pleasing balance in the room. Linked by color, the bold paisley and plaid work harmoniously together.

Florals, checks, and plaids often work beautifully with one another. In this case, color, again, is the unifying element. For extra pop, the coral-color headboard echoes one of colors in the floral print.

STEP 1 develop your palette

Bringing to bear all you now know about color (how it affects mood, how it can seemingly expand or decrease space, what you like, and what your family likes), pick one. Frequently, you can establish your color based on elements already in the room that you don't plan to replace—an upholstered furnishing, a carpet, or even a favorite painting.

Once you determine the main color, look at its complement or triad on the color wheel, and pick an accent or two. Go to the paint store, and get sample chips of each of your colors in every intensity you can find.

STEP 2 accent with pattern

Geometric patterns often mix well together—stripes with checks or plaids or dots. It is always easier to mix patterns that contain one or more common colors. Other links can be fabric weight, texture, and degree of formality. You can mix patterns in different scales. Use a large pattern on a large element, such as a sofa, smaller prints for windows, and something smaller still for pillows. Same-size patterns fight for attention. As a general rule, a good mix includes small-, medium-, and large-scale prints. Checks with stripes, dots with plaids, and florals with geometrics are all possibilities.

In Touch with Texture

The easiest way to incorporate texture into a design is with fabric. Brocades and damasks, moirés and chenilles, tweeds, and chintzes—all conjure up different looks and sensations. Fabrics, however, are just the beginning. Tactile interest can emanate from any material or surface that is coarse or smooth, hard or soft, matte or shiny. Coarse and matte surfaces, such as stone, rough-hewn wood, stucco, corduroy, or terra-cotta, absorb light and sound. Glossy and smooth surfaces, which range from metal and glass to silk and enamel, reflect light. Rugs, hard furnishings, wallcoverings, flooring, and accessories can add the texture your design needs.

The texture of scuffed wood and cane chair backs offers an interesting contrast to a smooth stone floor, left.

A grasscloth-like wall-covering adds "touch" to a wall, left, without the delicacy and care needs of the material in its natural form.

go green

BETTER BREATHING

Today you can find eco-friendly wallcoverings that are manufactured with "green" options, such as water-based inks that do not contain formaldehyde and other harmful components, such as volatile organic compounds (VOCs) that can make you ill.

Skin and fur look-alikes are often used for decorating. This alligator-skin effect, right, is actually a textured wallcovering.

1 global palettes

6 urban hues

the top **10**
Color Trends

1 **global palettes** Color expert Amy Wax says that paint manufacturers are embracing other cultures and places by creating palettes that invoke their aesthetic, such as the rich colors of India or the warm hues of desert sands. These new colors also open up a world of possibilities as accent hues for the color shy.

2 **"organic" colors** These are the colors schemes that are inspired by natural materials. They're not as intense as some of the colors in the global palette, says Wax, and are in the "safe zone" where people feel comfortable. Colors include stone, beige, gray, taupe, and terra-cotta.

8 super-deep colors

3 high-gloss finishes Interior designer Lucianna Samu reports that gloss is in—whatever you are painting—particularly in white.

4 saturated aqua greens These are on Samu's list of newly trending colors. She also cites what she calls, "crazy ramped-up turquoise" as the new "it" color.

5 simplicity This approach to creating a color palette includes soft, understated colors paired with clean white trim. It is for rooms intended for relaxing.

6 urban hues These colors are inspired by concrete and metal. Amy Wax says that these colors are more dramatic and sophisticated than earth tones.

7 color up top No more ignoring the fourth wall, look for color on ceilings, says Lucianna Samu. Sometimes it can be a subtle hint.

8 super-deep colors Dark and cozy, this paint palette features deep, dark hues, such as chocolate brown, that make you feel as if you've been wrapped up in a big, warm hug.

9 bold-color trimwork Doors and casings painted in a blast of contrasting color can add an unexpected color boost.

10 blue and white This is a classic combination that returns to the decorating scene often and is once more in vogue.

chapter 4

about furniture

How you furnish your home makes an impression on visitors who can learn something about your personal style—formal, casual, traditional, contemporary, and so forth—in a glance. But more importantly, the furniture choices you make affect your comfort, both physical and visual. And so, knowing your needs, considering your budget, and choosing pieces designed to last is the formula to follow whether you are purchasing big-ticket items or accent pieces.

Furniture for everyday or occasional use
should share the same criteria when you shop—
quality should be your top priority.

2 handmade, one of a kind

the top 10
Trends in Home Furnishings

1 quality Cheap, throwaway furniture is out; built-to-last pieces are back and here to stay.

2 handmade, one-of-a-kind The Internet has provided worldwide access to the work of new designers and craftspersons.

4 retro

10 pattern

3 informal elegance Nesting, a byproduct of the weak economy, calls for furniture that is comfortable, lighthearted, and laid-back.

4 retro Retro furniture continues to inspire designers. In addition, mixing old and vintage-inspired pieces with contemporary designs is a trend.

5 bye, bye minimalist Well, not entirely, but severe Modern design seems to be giving way to a more lived-in, inviting look.

6 natural, organic materials This is especially true in terms of paint and fabric. Interior designer Barbara Winfield states, "As designers become more aware of ecological challenges in the home furnishings industry, there is a move toward natural materials. It has become chic to be environmentally responsible."

7 better storage Controlling clutter, says Winfield, not completely eliminating it, appears to be the way of today. But do so with style. "The idea is to create elegant clutter," she says. "Organizing products and pieces are now designed to be both attractive and functional."

8 indoor/outdoor Furniture designers and manufacturers continue to blur the line between indoor and outdoor furnishings as the popularity of outdoor living shows no sign of winding down.

9 metallics and glass Metallic finishes on casegoods and textiles, along with glass and mirror surfaces, are adding a luxe look to the home.

10 lots of pattern Furniture-industry experts say that pattern is coming on strong. Look for influences from nature and folk art that originates in cultures spanning the globe.

Seating

Sofas come in all shapes and sizes. Two-seaters are sometimes called "love seats." Other sofa terms are **Chesterfield** (overstuffed, tufted upholstery with padded arms), **Lawson** (arms lower than the back), and **tuxedo** (arms the same height as the back). Backs of sofas can be camel back, channel back, or tufted back, all of which are firm, spring-supported styles. Pillow backs are available as either attached or loose. Base treatments include skirts, upholstered legs, plinth (block) bases, and bun feet.

Club and **wing chairs** are popular upholstered styles. A barrel chair has a rounded back that extends in a smooth line with the arms. Occasional chairs are characterized by wooden or metal arms and legs that are combined with seats and backs that are sometimes upholstered.

Modular seating comes in any number of armless units, single-arm end modules, and corner pieces that can be arranged in various configurations to suit different spaces and needs.

＊do this...not that

great divide

In a large open plan that needs defined areas, rather than placing a low-back sofa against the wall, move it into the room to divide the space. This creates a separation between the spaces but does not close them off from one another or block natural light.

A club chair and ottoman, opposite top, provide comfortable seating for reading or watching TV. A classic wing chair, left, is a favorite of fans of traditional style. A sleek Modern sofa and leather-and-chrome side chairs, below, are at home with clean-lined mid-century Modern architecture.

A neutral palette on the walls and furnishings creates a calm elegance in this living room, which is not exactly casual but far from stuffy and formal.

Far right: The sofa's exposed legs, a contemporary detail, keeps the look light and fuss-free. The antique accent chair adds a graceful note.

Top right: Upon a closer look, notice the tone-on-tone scroll pattern in the sofa's fabric that adds interest to the piece and echoes the pretty arms on the chair.

it's in the
details *

Bottom right: The glass-and-metal coffee table adds a luxurious accent to the room.

about furniture

Upholstery FAQs

Four elements determine the integrity of upholstered furniture: the frame, the springs, the cushions, and the upholstery fabric. High-quality **frames** are made of seasoned hardwood, kiln-dried to resist warping. The frame is joined using dowels and corner blocks that are screwed and glued together. Legs should be extensions of the frame and not attached with screws. Center legs add additional support.

The **spring systems** in upholstered furniture are either hand-tied coils or sagless (sinuous) constructions. Eight-way hand-tied springs are of the highest quality. Sagless springs are S-shaped, have a firmer feel than coil springs, and are often used in pieces that are lower to the floor.

A good frame is padded with cotton or polydacron so that the upholstery fabric never touches the wood. Quality **seat cushions** and **loose back cushions** combine down and other feathers wrapped around a polyurethane foam core—or loose down or feathers for back cushions. Test the quality of a cushion by lifting it. If it feels light, it may be made of poor materials.

Before buying furniture, examine it for quality. Sturdy arms, left, are a good sign. Check the back and underneath. These chairs, above, have a strong frame made from kiln-dried hardwood. Hand-tied springs and down and other-feather cushions, opposite, make this seating comfortable and durable.

Back cushions are supported by springs or webbing. If they are loose as opposed to attached, there are no springs. Webbing will supply the only support. This type of construction is less expensive than attached cushions and will feel less resilient.

Upholstery fabric comes in a range of price levels, called "grades," of fabric or coverings that are assigned a letter from A to D, with A at the high end. Grading is determined by the quality of the materials, the amount of fabric needed for a good match of the pattern, and the source of the pattern design. An important factor is durability. In general, tightly woven fabrics wear best. Fabrics with woven-in patterns wear better than printed fabrics. Various natural and synthetic fibers offer different looks and textures as well as cleanability and wearability performance.

Durable, easier-to-clean synthetic fibers have been developed as alternatives to natural fibers and are often blended with them.

Words of caution: never judge the quality of an upholstered piece solely by the fabric. The fabric can be easily replaced, but the frame and support system cannot.

Perfect for nesting, attractive, comfortable furniture suits today's lifestyle.

Right: There is nothing fussy, but there is plenty of flair, giving this sofa the sort of appeal that's right for simply relaxing or for entertaining guests.

Opposite top: A plush club chair is lively in a bold print that complements the warm solid-orange color of the sofa's natural cotton fabric.

Opposite bottom: A collection of throw pillows in sunny yellow and cheerful

it's in the
details *

greens carries the casual theme along, while the blue-and-white pillow provides a visual link from the sofa to the chair.

find patterned textiles
@ www.kravet.com
www.kathrynireland.com

about furniture

Solid-wood construction, as featured in the dresser above, is most desirable, especially when it is a hardwood such as oak. A high-quality wood cabinet, opposite, is a versatile storage piece that can house everything from clothing and linens to electronic equipment.

Casegoods and Tables

Casegoods is the term that refers to any piece of furniture used for storage. The furniture industry uses a variety of labels to denote the construction materials for casegoods. The meanings of these labeling terms are regulated by the Federal Trade Commission. They are as follows:

- **Solid wood** (i.e., "solid oak" or "solid pine") means that the exposed surfaces are made of solid wood without any veneer or plywood. Other woods may be used on unexposed surfaces, such as drawer sides and backs.
- **Genuine wood** means that all exposed parts of the furniture are constructed of a veneer of a type of wood over hardwood plywood.
- **Wood** means all of the parts of the furniture are made of some type of wood.
- **Man-made materials** refers to plastic laminate panels. The furniture may also include molded plastic that mimics wood panels, carving, or trim.

Tables can be made of any of the above materials, as well as metal, glass, and stone.

You pretty much get what you pay for, so look for strong construction at the joints, avoiding anything that is held together by staples only.

Quality Checks

When shopping for wood furniture you'll find varying levels of quality and pricing. Keep in mind that when it comes to furniture frames, veneers and laminates should be securely joined to the base material, and joints that bear weight should be reinforced with corner blocks. Back panels should be screwed into the frame, and long shelves should have center supports.

Check all drawers, making sure that they fit well, glide easily, and have stops. Drawer bottoms should be held by grooves in the drawer frame, not staples or nails, and interiors should be smooth and sealed.

If you're buying an armoire or wood cabinet, doors should open and close smoothly, and hinges and other hardware should be strong and secure.

Finally, all finishes should feel smooth unless they are intentionally distressed or crackled.

go green

RECLAIMED WOOD

Many manufacturers are using reclaimed wood—reclaimed lumber or wood salvaged from old furniture and houses—and turning it into new pieces. Look for the Smart-Wood Rediscovered label.

Exposed wood on an upholstered piece, below, should have a smooth finish. To enhance looks and durability, the finish on this dining set, opposite, has been sealed.

Q+A

I'm thinking of purchasing a leather sofa. Is that a practical idea? Can you offer some advice about care?

what the experts say

Experts at Sofa-Guide.com say, "Wear of your new sofa can be accelerated by dust and dirt. Regular cleaning of your leather sofa will keep it looking great. In most cases, all that is needed to clean your leather sofa is a damp cloth. Avoid using chemical cleaning agents or spray polishes, as these are not necessary and can damage the leather finish.

"Leather is susceptible to dye transfer, which is more noticeable on lighter colors of leather. Avoid sitting on your sofa with wet clothing, particularly denim as this usually has a high dye content. Leaving newspapers on the arms of a leather sofa is another example of how dye transfer may occur.

"Keep sharp objects such as keys or scissors away from your sofa, as leather can be easily scratched or cut. A cut or scratch in your leather sofa can be very noticeable and expensive to fix.

"If you do happen to spill liquid on your leather sofa, use paper towels to blot the affected area until dry. Do not rub, as this can cause discoloration or remove the leather finish.

"Avoid sitting in the same place all the time and sitting on the edge of cushions, as this can cause them to become misshapen and increases wear.

"Draw curtains or blinds during the day. Direct sunlight will make the color fade.

"Finally, keep your sofa away from strong heat sources, which can cause the leather to dry up and crack."

Some types of leather upholstery come with a top coating that adds luster to the material.

Bringing a sense of the outdoors into this living room was the goal of the designer. She accomplished it through the colors and textures in the furnishings.

Far right: The pale-green and cream upholstery fabrics look fresh surrounded by sunlight in this space.

Top right: Another visual link in the furnishings is created with pattern. Notice the similar motifs on the curtains, the cushions, the side table, and

it's in the details ✱

even the lamp.

Bottom right: An ottoman/coffee table in a natural woven material adds another element that links this interior with outdoor spaces.

about furniture

Furniture Facelifts

Y ou can help the environment and save money by using what you have or what you might find in Grandma's attic or an antique fair. It's not always difficult or expensive to give an old piece a facelift. Slipcovers, some reupholstery, a restored finish, and repurposing older pieces in new ways can add a lot of charm to your home, as can the juxaposition of old and new. In fact, most professional designers would advise you to avoid too much matching and recommend a little more mixing.

Paint is the obvious go-to when you want to update just about anything. Have an old chest of drawers that looks down and out? Apply a chic metallic finish. Turn boring to beautiful with color. Want to spray-paint your dining room chairs race-car red? Do it.

Slipcovers, opposite, are a versatile option for a new look. Reupholstering updates a vintage chair, above, while upholstering a headboard, below, adds a fresh change.

smart steps Choose Wisely

STEP 1 examine existing pieces

Look at what you have. Is it functional? Sturdy? Is refinishing or repurposing it an option? Can it be cost-effectively repaired or updated? Do you have special items, such as artwork or family heirlooms, that you'd like to blend with new furnishings?

Make a note of what you would like to keep and what pieces you think you may want to replace, either now or in the future. If you're on a tight budget, plan furniture purchases for which you might be able to save in the meantime.

STEP 2 consider lifestyle needs

Do you have young children or pets? Do you spend a lot of time at home, or are you always coming and going? Do you entertain frequently? How do you entertain, with a backyard barbecue or a formal sit-down dinner? Be smart: don't buy delicate upholstered pieces for the kids to flop on with the dog. Sometimes it makes sense to put fine things on hold and shop for something durable. Reconsider delicate fabrics or at least think about whether you can afford to have them professionally cleaned routinely.

STEP 3 stick with quality

It makes no sense to replace a well-crafted piece of furniture that might have a few dings in it just for the sake of having something new—especially if what you're buying is of lesser quality. Trends come and go, quality is never out of style.

If you must buy new, shop for furniture that will stand the test of time—both structurally and style-wise. Avoid designs that you know are of the moment and trendy colors and prints that will date your furniture and your home faster than you can say, "I'm over it."

STEP 4 reconsider reupholstery

Yes, we've said, "repurpose old pieces," but there are times when reupholstering furniture is not a good idea. These include

■ **When you think it's cheaper than buying new.** Not really. In fact, reuphostering a piece can cost as much or more than something new. Only reupholster furniture that is of high quality. Throw out the rest; it's junk.

■ **When you think you can do it yourself.** Not a good idea. Reupholstering is an art that uses special techniques. Find a professional; visit their shop; and get references.

window style

- ◆ FUNCTIONAL FLAIR
- ◆ SIZE AND PROPORTION
- ◆ FABRICS ◆ MEASURING
- ◆ SPECIAL TOUCHES
- ◆ IT'S IN THE DETAILS
- ◆ SHADES ◆ BLINDS AND SHUTTERS
- ◆ VALANCES ◆ HARDWARE
- ◆ PROBLEM SOLVING

First you have to decide how your window treatment has to function. Then it's on to the fun stuff, exploring your style options along with the practical considerations of the architecture of your windows and their size and placement. Maintenance and budget are part of planning, too, as are taking correct measurements and selecting the right hardware. Will you go the custom route, seeking professional design and installation help, or will you take on the job yourself?

You can't choose the right window treatments without considering the windows themselves. That's especially true in a room such as this one, which gets a lot of natural light.

Functional Flair

Window treatments do so much for a room. Besides adding style, they let you control the amount of natural light permitted into the room at various times of the day, limit summer heat gain and winter heat loss, and provide privacy where necessary. But you can also camouflage architectural blunders, create a focal point for a room, and enhance your decorating scheme with the right choice.

Fabric shades in a lightweight linen, opposite, filter light. Blinds, right, easily adjust to control light, air, and privacy. Custom shutters, below, are versatile and add an architectural element.

Modern Looks

In a modern or contemporary interior with a focal point, windows become part of the background, blending into the walls and allowing the star element to shine. Simple fabric draperies, blinds, or even bare windows (depending on your functional needs) will do. The color should match in hue or tone (intensity) with the surrounding walls for a clean, seamless look.

If your windows are the focal point in a modern setting, however, the treatment should be clean and simple, but with something to draw the eye, such as brilliant color in an otherwise neutral setting.

Shoji screens, opposite, which are translucent and slide from side to side, are a perfect choice for a modern Zen decor. Simple woven shades, above, suit the informal dining room in this contemporary home. Horizonal stripes on curtain panels, top right, update this living room, while tailored Roman shades look neat in this home office, bottom right.

Traditional Looks

Traditional interiors usually have a focal point, such as a fireplace, and so the windows may act as a secondary focal point or third-level spot of interest. If that is the case, downplay the window treatment but balance the room by adding substance and detail, perhaps with hardware, that will link the windows visually or thematically to the main focal point. Also, keep in mind that although all traditional and period styles have details specific to them, the modern take is to give a nod to tradition but to simplify it.

Saving Grace

When the windows necessitate custom-made treatments, possibly involving many yards of expensive fabric, you'll naturally gravitate toward more conservative choices to prevent an expensive mistake. However, this doesn't preclude using color, texture, or pattern to enrich your room. Let's say you've decided that a simple cream-colored curtain will function best in the space you're decorating. You still have the option of using a tone-on-tone vertical-stripe damask to add texture and pattern.

This window's layered treatment, opposite, features balloon shades and pinchpleat panels that have been pulled back with a tasseled cord. A heavy, lined fabric trimmed with silk tassels and slightly skimming the floor, above, creates a dramatic traditional look.

STEP 1 assess window style

The first thing to do is examine the achitectural style of the window. The most common types are

■ **Double-hung.** With two sash that move up and down, double-hungs are typical of traditional styles.

■ **Casement.** Contemporary-style casement windows are hinged vertically and swing in or out.

■ **Awning.** Also contemporary in design, awning windows are hinged horizontally and swing in or out.

■ **Sliding.** Top and bottom tracks allow sliders to glide from side to side.

In addition, there are special "architectural" windows.

STEP 2 assess function

What do you need the window treatment to do? What is the room's function?

For example, a bedroom requires a window treatment that is adjustable, allows light and air control, and provides privacy and perhaps insulation, whereas a window over the kitchen sink may only be decorative.

Don't forget, you can also choose a treatment to create a focal point in a room, set style, add color or pattern to a scheme, and disguise or enhance a window's architectural features. For problem-solving tips and examples, see pages 150-153.

STEP 3 make note of the sun

It's important to consider the room's orientation to the sun and the time of day that you use the room. This will tell you when you need to control natural light and whether you need a window treatment with insulating properties—particularly if the room faces north, which means it receives no direct sunlight. During cold-weather months, this room will be cold.

On the other hand, if the room faces south, it will get hot because it receives direct sunlight throughout the day. In this case, also consider a fabric that is treated to resist fading.

STEP 4 consider maintenance

Having window treatments professionally cleaned and reinstalled by an expert can be costly, so take that into account when making your plans if you are going the custom route; complex designs often require special skills because the window treatment is constructed on the window itself.

Some types of standard or ready-made window treatments also require dry cleaning or special care. Always check out the care instructions before buying, particularly if the curtain panels have an insulating backing or if the fabric is delicate.

Size and Proportion

Window treatments can do a lot to change the apparent size of your windows, making them seem larger or smaller and balancing an odd assortment of sizes and shapes to produce a more coherent effect. Your eye will register the size and shape of the treatment rather than that of the window.

For example, long panels can make short windows appear taller. Or when windows in a room are different sizes, de-emphasize the difference using curtains that are all the same length.

Installing the rod just below the ceiing adds grandeur to this design, left, while a band of rings separating the upper and lower portion of the curtains, below, balances the height of the windows with the scale of the room.

do this... not that

window too small?

Position the curtain rod above the window trim, or install floor-length panels. If you tie back the panels, more of the glass will be exposed. Another tip: install a pole that is wider than the window so that when the panels are drawn back, most of the glass is exposed. Treat multiple, consecutive units on a wall with panels or blinds that sweep across all of them to give the impression of one expansive window.

A somewhat small window becomes a focal point thanks to a curtain that extends beyond the frame and sill of the window.

A botanical-inspired print fabric softens the strong architecture of this large window bay, above.
This Near East-inspired heavy linen is suitable for drapery and fabric shades, opposite.

Fabrics

Curtains should drape smoothly, pleat well, and have body, so it's important to know something about the fabric. The weight of the fabric affects the finished appearance, too. Sheers soften the shape of a window treatment, while opaque fabrics add form. Prints and patterns create visual variety.

Fabrics that are recommended for window treatments include brocade, chenille, chintz, cotton, damask, and velvet. For something lighter, there's lace, linen, and silk. All are made from natural fibers. More-affordable and less-delicate fabrics are a blend of natural and synthetic fibers.

get smart
AVOID SUN DAMAGE
Sun damages all fabric, unless it is treated. However, a lining will slow the damaging effects considerably, as will sheer panels or blinds between the window and the curtain panels.

Solids versus Patterns

Window treatments give you the opportunity to add color, pattern, and texture to a room. If there is already pattern in the room, consider adding more with the window treatment. Multiple patterns balance each other. The secret to making this work is to change the scale. For example, a large-flowered chintz on the sofa will look great with a narrow stripe on the curtains and a medium plaid on side chairs. Just be sure to use patterns that have some colors in common.

Stripes, right, elongate a curtain. When panels are stacked to the side, below, notice how subtle the pattern becomes.

A bold, large-scale design such as this, above, has a big impact on a room.

Care and Maintenance

For elaborate draperies, monthly vacuuming will be sufficient, and expensive, time-consuming dry cleaning may be necessary only every three years or so. But this would be inadequate in a family room or even a master bedroom where children and pets are welcome visitors. Dusting and vacuuming are also suitable methods for cleaning hard treatments such as shutters and blinds.

Depending on the fabric, you may be able to launder simple curtains and valances. But don't forget: you will have to iron and rehang them. Dry cleaning is the most costly form of maintenance, especially if the size of the treatment calls for professional removal and remounting.

go green

ALLERGIES
Dust mites and pollen are common triggers of allergies. A few tips include
- *Keep the window treatments simple for easy cleaning.*
- *Avoid lined fabrications that require dry cleaning.*
- *Use sheer panels with unlined cotton panels for easy washing.*
- *Choose hard treatments, such as blinds and shutters, which are easy to dust.*

Wash sheers using a gentle detergent, and leave them to hang dry.

Measuring

Measure your windows accurately using a retractable metal tape. For a window treatment you plan to install inside the window frame, such as shades, shutters, and blinds, measure from the side of one casing to the other to determine the width. Then measure the length from the top of the frame to the sill.

For outside-mount treatments, measure the width of the window from the outer edge of the trim on one side to the other. For the length, measure from the top of the window trim to the sill. However, for curtains, measure from where you will install the rod to where your curtain will end—at the sill or lower.

Velvet panels, opposite, should measure two and one-half to three times the width of the rod. When these curtains, below, are closed, there should be enough fullness for them to hang in folds.

Special Touches

Window trimmings, tie-backs, and other special details are what will make even a ready-made window treatment look professionally designed. You might consider adding some type of embellishment—trim, tassels, beads, or fringe—to a plain curtain panel or shade for a custom look at a fraction of the price. Or look for something decorative to use as a tieback—a large tassel, cording, beads, or ribbons, to name a few.

Piping, banding, or braid are ways to finish or neaten edges or add a graphic line to a plain treatment, especially when the trim is in a contrasting color, print, or texture.

Trim, Fringe, and Tassels

Passementerie, or tassels and trimmings, encompass a range of beautiful interlaced, braided, and fringed decorations that have been used traditionally to enhance window treatments. Passementerie varies in quality and in price, and it is made by hand or machine. The type of thread used—silk, linen, viscose, or cotton—also influences cost. Here is a tiny sample of the vast array of styles and colors.

An unusual edge treatment in a contrasting color or fabric gives a plain curtain panel a special look.

Cotton fringe sewn along the vertical edge of a curtain, top, adds a finishing touch. Silk cord in a contrasting color makes an elegant tieback, bottom.

Special Touches **137**

Soft colors and fabrics create a soothing atmosphere in this guest room.

Far right: Lined Roman shades over lightweight side-gathered London shades are all that this room requires for light control and privacy at the windows. The Roman shades' fabric perfectly matches the drapery at the head of the bed and on the cornice.

Top right: A bejeweled hemline on the Roman shades adds feminine appeal.

it's in the
details ✳

The beads pick up the tones in the paisley motif of the London shade.

Bottom right: If the sun becomes too strong for an afternoon nap, a tug on the cord lowers the window treatment.

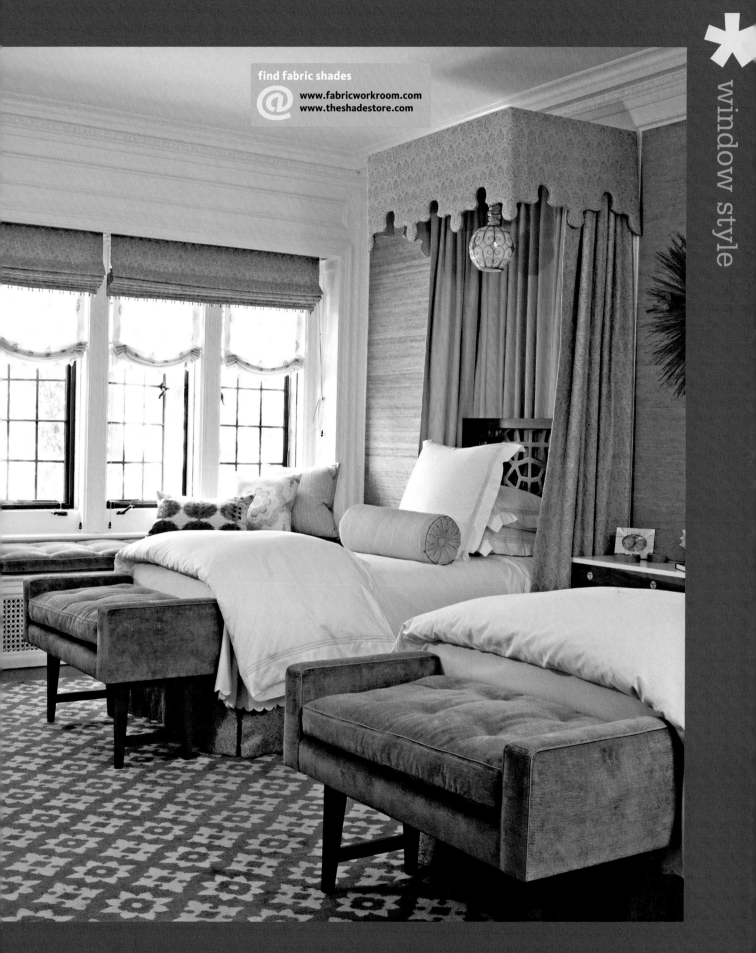

window style

Bottom-mounted lightweight pleated shades, left, offer privacy without obscuring light and views. Unlined linen Roman shades installed just below the transoms, below, provide partial sun screening. A woven "wood" shade, opposite top, can be fabricated from bamboo or other types of grass.

Shades

Shades are versatile; they can block out the light entirely or simply filter it. Use them alone for a casual look. Or pair them with a valance or swag. Popular variations include

- **Roman shades.** Sleek with flat, horizontal pleats.
- **Balloon shades.** Gathered fabric that billows or fans.
- **Pleated fabric shades.** Lightweight pleats that stack tightly.
- **Cellular shades.** Pleated fabric construction resembling a honeycomb.

Wood shutters with wide louvers, above, add an architectural element to a room. They offer the utmost control of light, air, and privacy. But traditional blinds, opposite top, do a good job, too. Pair either of these hard treatments with a curtain or valance to soften their looks.

Blinds and Shutters

Today's blinds—available in metal, wood, or vinyl—include many colors and some textures. You can choose vertical or horizontal slats in standard, mini, or micro widths. Contrasting tapes are available to create interesting decorative details.

Louvered shutters are available in some standard window sizes and as custom designs. Open them for air; close them for privacy; pair them—or not—with a fabric treatment. Some types come with a fabric panel that can be coordinated with other furnishings.

do this... not that

diffused light

Sliding Shoji screens are an elegant, understated way to focus attention on the windows in the room. They are a logical choice for an Asian- or Zen-inspired interior. You can also adopt this idea as an alternative to treating a sliding door.

*What's the best way to dress a pair of
French doors? Curtains can get in the way.*

what the experts say

Interior designer Nancee Brown, ASID, says "If
the door opens out, a valance or cornice may be
mounted at the top of the frame. If the door opens
in, these headers are a possibility only if there is
enough room to mount them on the wall above
the door. Treatments that can be secured directly
above and below the glass and curtains that stack
back tightly work well. If there is little wall space
on either side of the opening, don't use a heavy
fabric or a gathered curtain with a lot of fullness.
If you are using a swag, check that it doesn't drape
too low across the top where it can get caught in
the door.

"Shutters on tracks are a lovely choice, but they
require substantial stack-back space."

144 Chapter 5 WINDOW STYLE

These curtain panels slide easily across the metal rod, providing access to the doors.

Valances

While a valance does not contribute to privacy or light control, it does offer a way to add color and interest to a window or visually balance a layered treatment. A valance is generally 10 to 16 inches long, but it should be in proportion to the window. Valances with swoops or folds of fabric may be a few inches longer.

There are many valance styles. A triple-pleat valance, right, is pleated at the top and then released into soft folds. This swag and cascade jabot valance, below, features fan-folded ruffles that are arranged on top of each other in a narrow stacked pattern.

A simple gathered valance is an attractive top treatment over shutters, above. A more structured design, right, is the pelmut—an upholstered board that can be shaped in different ways and used with another window treatment or alone to make its own statement.

Hardware

The right hardware is important for supporting your curtains and draperies. A track system is the easiest type of drapery hardware to operate. It's typically hidden in the curtain heading or behind a valance. Some hardware is decorative as well as functional. Choose a style that matches the curtains or the room's decor.

Handsome hardware is part of the show today. It includes decorative rods, below left, and holdbacks, below right, to complement your design.

Match your metals. Brass grommets with a satin finish coordinate seamlessly with this curtain rod, left. This "shephard's crook" holdback, below, in wrought iron was inspired by the curlicue pattern in the fabric.

Problem Solving

There are some situations that make choosing a window treatment tricky business. Included are windows in the same room but of different sizes, windows that are too large or too small, and awkwardly shaped or situated windows, such as those that are too close to the ceiling or in a corner. Other difficult-to-treat windows might include special shapes, such as ovals, circles, half-rounds, and elipses.

Here are some of the common situations that homeowners find vexing in terms of window treatments.

Do you have one window that is taller than another? Align the curtain rods, top left. Combine style and utility with Roman shades for small units high on a wall, bottom left. Large windows in tall rooms can be hard to dress. In this bedroom, above, drapes and shutters provide privacy while untreated transoms admit light.

Fabric is the unifying element here, and another way to dress windows of different sizes.

This swag design, top left, balances the need for softness without obscuring a beautiful window. Tailored shades have been installed on the staggered windows' frieze boards below the molding in this office, top right. An hourglass sheer installed with tension rods is a pretty idea for this small fixed window, right.

Once again, fabric comes to the rescue to unite openings of different sizes, such as the French door and double-hung window at top left and the two windows at top right. A sunburst sheer is the perfect solution for this fixed unit, left.

walls 101

Wondering what to do with a blank wall? Stop staring at it, and consider some of the ideas in this chapter. You'll find examples of using fine art and framed prints (and how to hang and arrange them), mirrors, clocks, and textiles to create interesting displays. In addition, you'll also find great ways to use wall treatments and trimwork, paneling, paint (and its special effects), and the latest wallpapers.

The bold color of the walls is enhanced in this bedroom by an artful display on the walls.

I'm at a loss about what to do with my plain beige walls. They look boring blank, but I'm afraid of making a mistake.

what the experts say

Interior designer Lynn LoCascio, Allied NJASID, says don't be afraid to hang art or other items of interest on a wall.

"It's all about proportion," states LoCascio. That means finding something that is the right size for the wall and whatever furniture that may be against it.

"Wall art is a major aspect in the history of interior design," LoCascio adds. "In addition to framed paintings and photography, there is a plethora of items that can be used."

Some of the things to consider are collectibles—a grouping of old hats, a vintage piece of apparel, architectural salvage, everyday items of times long passed such as wooden bowls or rolling pins, odd pieces of china, and so forth.

"A plain wall comes alive with a well-balanced arrangement of strong, bright-colored images. Small pictures can be mounted with large mats, giving the images stature and perspective for a dramatic feel.

"When deciding how to address a wall, consider the furniture as well, which will form a link to the size and quantity of a grouping."

If wall art isn't in your budget, paint a feature wall an exciting color.

Face Value

The very size of a wall makes it an important element in your decor, but it's too often underused or treated badly. A wall can stand as a dramatic statement on its own or serve unobtrusively as a backdrop, letting the furnishings take center stage.

Color, pattern, and texture, accomplished with paint, wallcoverings, or trimwork, are just part of the picture, albeit an important part. Wall decor—paintings, framed prints or photographs, sculpture, textiles, architectural salvage used as objets d'art, and unique displays add so much to making a home interesting and warm as long as you know how to present and arrange them pleasingly—keeping in mind scale, proportion, balance, rhythm, and harmony.

All-white frames and matting unifies this display. This type of grouping only works if all of the elements are carefully measured, evenly spaced, and plumb.

Even in this age of telling time digitally, wall clocks continue not only as time keepers but as art. This one, left, is the focal point in a front hall.

Various textiles can be used as wall art, but they need to be properly mounted. Some keepsakes, such as this flag, right, require special preservation measures to protect them against pollutants and the sun's damaging UV rays.

Artful Living

Art shouldn't be treated as an afterthought in the design scheme. A large piece of art can influence your room's decor, as may collections. Consider these elements as you are designing the room. Art is shown to its greatest effect in uncluttered surroundings. A large modern painting has more impact if left alone on a wall; small- or medium-size items are more impressive grouped together.

If you are displaying drawings or photography, make sure that the frame is large enough to accom-

modate a mat. The frame should be 1 to 3 inches larger in dimension than the picture. For an up-to-date look, make the mat at least 6 inches larger than a photograph or an illustration; this can be an effective way to draw attention to a small piece of art or photography.

There's strength in numbers, so group small items together on a wall for maximum effect, opposite far left. Vibrant hues in the oil paintings stand out against these cocoa-color walls, left. A built-in wall unit comprises shallow shelves, above, and provides display space for a collection of artifacts and antique books.

Frames

Frames should coordinate with but not necessarily duplicate any other frames used in the room. Unless you're making a statement with the juxtaposition, the frame style should also reflect the overall look of the room.

When buying a frame, examine the quality of the material from which it is constructed. Does it feel flimsy? Make sure that there aren't any gaps at the joints (the mitered corners of the frame). What is the condition of the finish? There shouldn't be any flaking or discoloration of metal frames or wood frames with a metallic finish, such as gold leafing. The finish on wood should be smooth and blemish free…unless you prefer vintage frames or ones with the look of age. In that case, imperfections are perfectly acceptable.

* do this…not that

mat first

Not all art requires using a mat, but if you decide to do so, choose the matting before you choose the frame.

Consider the mat's width; if it's too small it may restrict the image, although a large picture doesn't necessarily require a wide mat.

When choosing matting for a print, try picking up accent colors from your decor. If you feel your accents don't work with the art, look at the room's main hue. You can also try a color that contrasts with the art. If all else fails, pick a neutral color from the work itself or a black or white mat.

"Frameless" picture frames made of thin plexiglass or plastic are perfect for posters and make a print such as this one, opposite top, appear to float on the wall. A collection of antique frames act as art on this wall, opposite bottom. Pictures arranged at eye level, above, are best.

smart steps Display with Flair

STEP 1 play with the elements

Before hammering a nail into the wall, place all of the art on the floor, and try out different arrangements. Or on plain paper, trace or draw to scale the items you want to hang; cut them out; and tape them onto the wall, rearranging until you've got it right.

A vertical grouping will make a wall seem higher; a horizontal one will make the room seem wider. Don't get stuck in a rut: you don't have to arrange everything in a row. A triangular shape might work for an end wall in a room with a cathedral ceiling; a rectangle or oval may fit in an area above a mantel or sofa.

STEP 2 check proportions

A framed piece that is too small will look insignificant over a large piece of furniture. The frame should be approximately two-thirds the size of the piece over which it hangs. If you still want to use the small piece, pair it with another that is approximately the same size.

When you're creating groupings of framed prints or paintings that vary in size, try to keep the weightier pieces on the bottom of the arrangement, or place two smaller elements next to it. A large piece will anchor the grouping and keep the arrangement from seeming top-heavy or from trailing off.

art arrangements

Don't get locked into arranging framed pieces in rows. Try imagining a circle for prints hung in an entry. Or let the shape of your walls influence the arrangement, such as a triangle for a gable wall. Even if you stay within the framework of a rectangle, pictures and objects in various sizes will keep the grouping from looking too rigid. Just make sure to balance the visual weight of the arrangement (bottom). A grid pattern works when you have different-size mats; the orderly rows unify the pieces (below left).

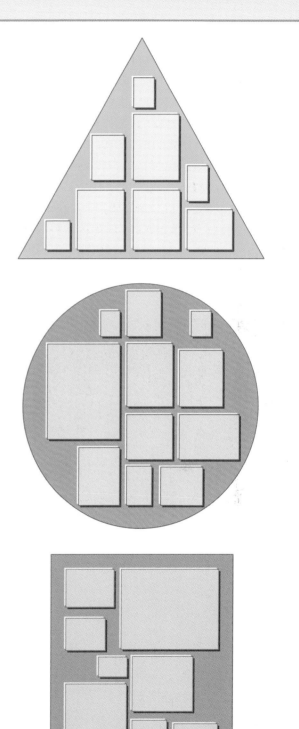

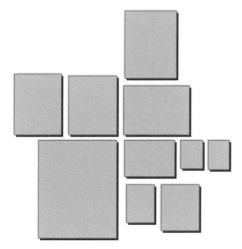

Mirrors

Capture views; open up a dark corner; visually elongate or widen a wall; or simply dress up a room with a beautiful mirror. There are mirrors to suit every style of decor. Create a focal point with a large framed mirror, or artfully group a collection of smaller ones of varying shapes and sizes on a wall. Mix and match mirrors in groupings with framed prints or paintings.

Mirrors offer a versatile option for dressing up a wall in any room. Strategically placed mirrors can reflect more natural light into a room.

In small quarters, below, a mirror acting as a headboard opens up a tight corner of space. The frame of a mirror is often quite decorative. This sunburst mirror, opposite top left, is one variation on the style. An ornate gold frame adds an extra touch of luxury to this design, opposite top right. Tall mirrors flanking a cabinet amplify the sense of space in this room, opposite bottom.

An over-scaled lattice effect dresses up a once-plain wall. The "panels" can be painted or upholstered.

Trim-Tastic

Decorative trim gives a room a finished appearance. An enormous variety of stock and specialty trim exists in a wide range of materials, including wood, plaster, and fiberglass.

At the top of a wall, crown molding can combine with other molding styles for an opulent look, or you can use simpler cove molding, which eliminates the ceiling line but doesn't stand out.

A frieze is a wide band that runs under the cornice but above the picture rail. As the name suggests, the picture rail is used to hang artwork. A chair rail is installed around the room, 30 to 35 inches from the floor, and is often used in conjunction with a wainscot, or waist-high paneling, on the lower portion of the wall.

Base moldings give the floor line a higher profile and can be as elaborate or as simple as you like.

A painted chair rail and base molding add an elegant touch to this hallway.

Handsome trimwork, such as this crown molding, adds value as well as decoration to a home.

Paneling and Wall Frames

Forget everything you remember about that fake wood paneling that was popular during the 1970s. Today's paneling is a stylish way to add authentic architectural character to a room.

Another way to do this is with wall frames—a series of large "picture frames" created with molding that add a raised pattern along any bare stretch of wall. Combined with a chair-rail molding and base trim, wall frames are elegant and sophisticated—and the perfect accent for a traditional decor. You can find do-it-yourself instructions online or in books.

White-painted paneling with picture-frame molding, above, has a formal appearance, while natural wood paneling on the wall of this beach-house bedroom, opposite, is more casual.

Painted scrolls over a lively green background perk up a dark hallway, above.
In a formal dining room, opposite, eggplant-color walls look dramatic.

The Power of Paint

Even if you prefer to give your walls just a standard coat of paint (always a dependable decorating strategy), you've got a wide range of colors from which to choose; even neutral hues come in a variety of shades and tones. Professional designers typically bring samples of the fabric and carpet to the paint store to have a custom color mixed to match. These paints are more expensive but are worth it. Even two shades of white can clash. (See Chapter Three, "Color," page 50.) Look at color samples with your furnishings in all types of light and at various times of the day. Buy a small amount of paint in several colors or shades to compare on the wall. To pull your interior design together, select a color that you can pick up from the upholstery or drapery fabric in either a matching or contrasting tone.

go green

ECO FRIENDLY

Conventional paints contain volatile organic compounds, commonly referred to as "VOCs," that are harmful to the environment, can irritate your eyes and lungs, and are toxic. Do yourself and the environment a favor and buy low- or zero-VOC paints.

Faux and Beyond

Using paint to create faux effects of natural materials, such as stone and wood, is a trend that has waxed and waned numerous times. Although many of these techniques are classics, today's most popular paint effects include **glazing,** a technique that involves applying a paint or colorant mixed with a transparent medium and a thinner to a surface, and **color washing,** which is coating a surface with a thinned-out latex or acrylic paint.

This wild design was created with stencils. When the homeowner tires of it, it will be a lot easier to remove (by painting over it) than wallpaper.

Rather than creating a faux effect, these techniques are really meant to add depth to a surface. If you want to try them yourself, practice first; otherwise, hire an expert to do it for you.

You might also explore what you can do with stencils, which are more sophisticated than ever, or with a wall mural. The latter should be left to a professional artist, however.

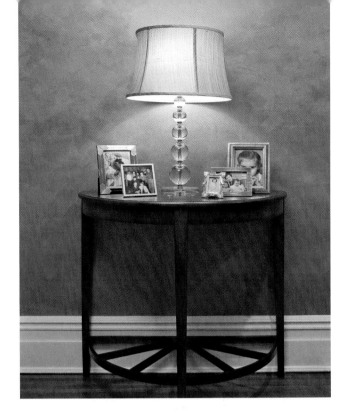

To create the rich-looking effect at right, a color wash was applied to a vibrant base coat. Although it is probably more elaborate than most people would choose to do, this mural, below, added drama where it was needed.

Versatile Wallpaper

t's rarely made of 100 percent paper today, but wallpaper is versatile, with many styles, colors, patterns, and textures from which to choose. It's certainly one way to re-create certain period looks and imitate delicate and costly natural materials.

The most common types of wallpaper are **fabric-backed vinyl,** which is durable and washable. It comes prepasted, as does **paper-backed vinyl,** which is not quite as tough but is washable. **Vinyl-coated paper** is inexpensive, but its thin protective coating tears easily and doesn't hold up well to dirt and stains.

This large-print wallpaper, left, designed in the 1960s, has become a classic in different colorways. Many wallpaper manufacturers offer coordinating fabrics, opposite.

Other Types of Wallcoverings

If you have extra to spend, there are special wallcoverings that will heighten the luxury factor of your decor.

■ **Foil Coverings:** Delicate foil wallpapers can make a room seem larger. But the surface of the wall must be very smooth because foil will magnify any of its imperfections. Professional installation is recommended.

■ **Flocked Coverings:** Featuring a raised, fuzzy pattern, flocked wallcoverings resemble expensive cut velvet.

They look at home with traditional or period interiors, but use them sparingly—they can be too ornate for most contemporary tastes.

■ **Natural Coverings:** Grass cloth, hemp, and other natural weaves bring texture to a room. Some are very delicate and require application over liner paper. They can also fray and are not washable. Professional installation is recommended.

■ **Embossed Coverings:** Lincrusta is a heavy linoleum-

like covering. Its embossed surface features stylized designs that simulate raised moldings made of wood, plaster, tile, or leather. Professional installation is recommended. Anaglypta, which is similar but cheaper and lighter, is made of cotton-fiber pulp. These two rich-looking, durable coverings can be painted and repainted several times over the years. They also camouflage imperfect walls. You can use them for an entire wall application or halfway up the wall, wainscot style.

The popularity of metallics has extended to wallcoverings. Totally unlike the foils popular during the 1970s, today's designs are more elegant and sophisticated. The floral motif on a metallic background, opposite, has a nostalgic look, while the classic pattern, below, has subtle glamour.

chapter 7
lighting

Knowing how much and what type of light you need for the various activities in your home is an important aspect of design. Yet light, in general, is often an afterthought. Don't get lost in the dark. It's really not that complicated to plan lighting for your home that goes beyond simply selecting attractive fixtures. Here's what you need to know to become enlightened.

Tiers of translucent natural shells soften the light coming from this capiz pendent.

The ability to control the levels of natural and artificial light is an important consideration when choosing fixtures and window treatments, above and opposite.

Natural and Artificial Light

The amount and quality of natural light a room receives depends on the size of its windows and its orientation with regard to the sun. South-facing windows get the lion's share of direct sunlight for most of the day. East-facing rooms benefit from early mornings, while rooms that face west are sunny in the afternoon. Because its back is to the sun, a north-facing room receives only indirect natural light and tends to be cool and dim.

When you are renovating or redecorating a room, always look at the existing space and take the seasons, time of day, and orientation of the windows into consideration with respect to natural light.

Artificial light picks up where natural light leaves off. It is the illumination that you provide, and unlike natural light, you can fine-tune it. In the daytime, artificial light augments natural light; after dark, it compensates for complete lack of daylight.

The key to devising a versatile plan that can change with each activity, as well as with the time of day or the weather, begins with knowing about the different types of artificial light.

A ceiling fixture such as this one, above, can provide good general lighting, depending on the size of the room.

Ambient Light

Ambient, or general, light is illumination that fills an entire room. Its source is sometimes an overhead fixture, but the light itself does not appear to come from any specific direction. The key to good ambient lighting is making it inconspicuous. It is merely the backdrop for the rest of the room, and it changes with the

surrounding environment—always providing light but never becoming obvious.

For example, ambient lighting used during the day should blend in with the amount of natural light entering the room. At night, you should be able to adjust the level of supplemental artificial light so that it doesn't contrast jarringly against the darkness outside.

Large spaces such as this family room, below, benefit from recessed fixtures that can provide an even spread of light throughout the room.

Task Light

As its name implies, task lighting is purely functional. It illuminates a specific area for a particular job, such as chopping food on a kitchen counter, reading a book, or applying makeup.

Lighting on both sides of a vanity mirror is an example of good task lighting. It provides cross-illumination while avoiding the distorting shadows often seen with overhead lighting.

Ideally, vanity lighting should be located at the side of the mirror, left. For reading propped up in bed, these fixtures, below, cast light slightly behind the readers' shoulders. In a kitchen, opposite, a track system offers versatile task lighting.

Accent and Decorative Light

Accent lighting creates a mood and shapes space. This particular type of lighting is sometimes overlooked but always appreciated. It calls attention to a particular element in a room, such as an architectural feature. For example, installed in a cove over a bathtub, the light shimmers above the water and delineates the bathing area dramatically.

Without accent lighting, there may be light—but no show business. Utilizing it, a design becomes exciting, theatrical, and rich.

While accent lighting draws attention to something specific, **decorative lighting** draws attention only to itself. Some types of decorative lighting include candles, neon sculptures or signs, or a strip of miniature lights.

Inside a glass-door cabinet, left, is an excellent place to install accent lighting. Spotlights in the soffit over the cabinet and cove lighting above the table, opposite, are two more examples of accent lighting.

do this... not that

not to be taken lightly

Don't overlook what you can do with light. Eyes are naturally drawn to the brightest element in the room. You can use this attraction to create visual tricks. At night, a light in the garden can visually extend a room to the outdoors, for example.

How Much Do You Need?

Good lighting begins with taking the recommended levels of light into account and tempering them with your preferences. In common spaces, such as the family room, living room, and kitchen, it is better to err on the side of brightness. Adapt lighting in private areas, such as a study, bedroom, or workshop, to individual needs or requirements.

To reduce glare from a lamp, adjust the angle of the fixture or use a low-wattage lightbulb or one with frosting. Also, make sure the bulb has the proper shade or cover—never leave it exposed.

go green

SAVE MORE

Using energy-saving light sources, such as compact fluorescent lamps (CFLs), is great, but to reduce costs and consumption even more, wire different fixtures to separate switches so that you can turn on only the one you need.

Low-heat pin-based, as opposed to screw-in, compact fluorescent lights, (CFLs) are a proper fixture for a closet, left. A lamp situated slightly behind and to the side of the chaise, above, is recommended for reading.

recommended ranges of light levels

You can avoid eyestrain by having plenty of ambient light, thereby reducing the contrast to task lighting. Start by determining the level of light needed for the activity or task, and then relate it to the surroundings. Task lighting, lighting immediately nearby, and then the lowest lighting in the area (as in a room's corners) should range from no more than a ratio of four to one, preferably three to one near task lighting. You can compare watts and foot-candles cast by various light sources to determine the ratios or approximate them with your naked eye.

The following table provides the recommended ranges of light levels for seeing activities in the home. The more intense the activity, the greater the light level should be.

ACTIVITY	EASY OR SHORT DURATION	CRITICAL OR PROLONGED
Dining	Low	Low
Entertaining	Low to high	Low to high
Grooming	Moderate	High
Craftwork*	Moderate	High
Kitchen/laundry chores	Low to moderate	High
Reading	Low to moderate	High
Studying	Moderate	High
TV viewing	Low to moderate	Low to moderate
Computer work	Moderate	High
Workbench*	Moderate	High
Tabletop games	Low to moderate	Moderate to high
Writing	Low to moderate	High

* Benefits from supplementary directional light.

Q&A

I'm unsure about the type of lampshade to use? Is there a difference?

what the experts say

Interior designer Lynn Peterson says, "Just as linen and lace curtains diffuse light, translucent fabric lampshades filter light while obscuring the naked bulb. On the other hand, opaque paper shades allow light to emerge solely from the openings of the top and bottom of the shade. They offer drama and will light whatever is underneath or above, but they don't glow the way translucent shades do. However, one advantage of dark or opaque shades is that they will not reflect back at you from windows at night or from the TV screen."

The most common mistake people make when buying a lampshade for a table lamp is choosing one that is too big for the lamp base. According to the experts at Lamps USA (www.lampsusa.com), there are a few rules of thumb:

- Shade height should be about ¾ the height of the base.
- The bottom of the shade should be wider than the widest part of the base.
- Shade width should approximately equal the height from the bottom of the base to the socket.

They also caution that you may need a larger harp if you are replacing a standard incandescent bulb with a compact fluorescent (CFL), which is taller.

Choosing a lampshade is about more than style. Here, a translucent shade casts a soft, diffused glow that sets the right mood.

How Much Do You Need? **193**

Lighting Fixtures

Fixtures have become more decorative and lighting schemes more varied and eclectic in recent years. Your whole-house lighting plan may run the gamut and include table and floor models, wall sconces, pendants and chandeliers, strip lights, recessed canister lights, track lights, and ceiling fixtures. They all come in copious finishes and styles that easily coordinate with any decor.

Recessed spotlights and vintage-inspired pendants are stylish and practical in this kitchen, left. In a large, open plan with a double-height-plus ceiling, right, pendants reminiscent of classic Noguchi lamps provide general lighting throughout the space.

A chandelier, right, can be a source of ambient and accent light. Install a dimmer for maximum light-level versatility.

The Hang of It

Avoid the mistake of hanging a light fixture too high or too low. Installing a chandelier? Depending on its size, hang a chandelier or pendant 30–34 inches above the top of a table or countertop—the larger the fixture, the higher it should hang. Install sconces on the wall 60 to 70 inches up from the floor. If you're using sconces above a mantel, position them at least 10 inches above the mantel shelf.

As a rule of thumb, the larger the light fixture, the higher you can hang a chandelier. The arrangement in the room, opposite, has struck an ideal balance. To avoid glare on the work surface, right, pendants hang high. Sconces, below, are situated at a good height above the mantel.

Q&A

Is it true that the standard lightbulb is becoming obsolete? What replaces it?

what the experts say

"The first incandescent lamp to be phased out in January 2012 is the 100-watt A lamp," says interior designer and lighting expert Darryl Tucker, ASID, CID. The lamp he is referring to is the standard incandescent lightbulb that everyone has been using since Edison invented it. But don't fret. "The halogen A lamp [bulb] is a very good replacement, as it has good color and is only slightly more expensive—but not as costly as compact fluorescent lamps (CFLs) with a screw-in base," adds Tucker. "And there are other negative issues regarding the CFLs: the quality and color of the light, manufacturer-exaggerated lamp-life claims, and [special] disposal procedures.

"Although the new LED screw-in [bulbs] are not the most desirable replacement at this point in time either, they are a good point source for task and accent lighting."

Because "very unique and creative designs are being developed by both manufacturers and artists, consumers are enjoying a diverse selection of decorative pendants, sconces, and task lamps" that make good use of the LED's small size. "The fixtures can be smaller, thinner, and even flat in some cases."

A combination of various types of light yields a sophisticated ambiance in this room.

Light Effects

Lighting can be a creative tool that adds a special look to any room in the house. It is helpful to consult with a professional designer who can guide you and who has knowledge of some of the more sophisticated fixtures and lightbulbs that are available for creating various effects. However, there are some simple effects you may want to consider on your own. In any case, always hire a licensed electrician to install any fixtures.

Wall washing is a dramatic effect that's easily created with spotlights or track lights. You can also use these fixtures to highlight architectural features or art. As for the latter, it's probably best to consult a professional who will recommend the right voltage to use.

The right fixture and bulb is important when lighting a display. In this case, pin spotlights offer the proper amount of brightness with good heat dissipation.

Recessed "eyeball" spotlights, above, can be aimed in any direction. Here, one of them is used decoratively to downlight a wall. To illuminate art installed on a stair wall, right, a designer used a low-voltage halogen track system.

get smart
SEE IT FIRST

Before making a major investment in a fixture or a lighting system, it's wise to see it in the store. That way, you can see whether it produces the effect that you are seeking or not. Don't hesitate to ask to see various fixtures lit so that you can compare them.

smart steps   Get It Right

STEP 1 evaluate your needs

Above all, your lighting design should enhance the way things function in your home. Try following a recipe or assembling something without good lighting. Tailor your lighting to each room's activities. In other words, task lighting will be critical in your kitchen, while the TV room may require more-controlled ambient lighting.

Take a look at the physical space during the day and at night. How much natural light does it get? Do the windows face north (no direct sunlight), east (strong morning sunlight), south (strong sunlight all day), or west (strong afternoon sunlight)?

STEP 2 sketch an informal plan

Make an informal drawing of the room's floor plan. Note where to place your general lighting first; then indicate where you'll need task lights. After you've noted every activity center for task lighting, decide where you want to install accent lighting. You might want some recessed fixtures over a countertop or piece of art. Maybe you want to highlight a tray ceiling or hand-painted tile. If you want to use accent lighting but don't know where it should go, look for the most interesting feature in the room. This exercise will be helpful when you're selecting fixtures or discussing lighting with a professional.

STEP 3 check codes and laws

Every municipality has its own codes regarding the placement of light and electricity around water. Before you purchase any light fixtures for the kitchen and bath, especially, check your local code with the building inspector or speak with your contractor.

If you haven't already replaced your incandescent bulbs with compact fluorescent lamps (CFLs), now is the time to do so or to select another type of energy-saving lighting, such as LED lamps. In some parts of the country, this has been the law for a number of years, and as of 2012 it is federally mandated.

STEP 4 visit showrooms

The best way to get ideas is to visit lighting showrooms and the lighting department in home centers. This will give you a chance to take an inventory of fixture types and styles currently on the market. Also, you can take advantage of the advice of lighting specialists employed at these stores. They can help you create the right plan and choose an appropriate fixture style. Bring along your sketch. As you might already expect, some in-store advice is free. A few suggestions may be all you need to steer you in the right direction. Otherwise, you may want to consider an in-home consultation.

chapter 8
floor style

- ◆ **WARM WOOD**
- ◆ **LAMINATES**
- ◆ **"GREEN" FLOORING**
- ◆ **TILE AND STONE**
- ◆ **RESILIENT VINYL**
- ◆ **CARPETS AND RUGS**

Your floor is another element in your design that can set the style and tone of your room. If you are redoing everything "from the floor up," so to speak, you may want to consider all of your options, from the ever-popular wood to laminate, "green" bamboo and cork, ceramic tile or stone, and resilient vinyl. Don't, however, forget about carpets and rugs. They are not only soft underfoot, but useful as another way to shape space and add color and pattern.

The contrast of a light-colored rug placed over a dark wood floor intensifies the rich deep tones in the wood.

Warm Wood

Wood varieties available as a flooring material are vast, and cost varies widely, depending on the type and grade of wood and the choice of design (strips or parquet).

Softwoods, such as pine and fir, are often used to make simple tongue-and-groove floorboards. These floors are less expensive than hardwoods but also less durable. Softwoods are not suitable for high-traffic areas, for rooms with heavy furniture (which can "dig" into the wood), or for kitchens or dining rooms, where chairs or other furniture will often be moved around. The **hardwoods**—maple, birch, oak, ash—are far less likely to mar with normal use. A hardwood floor is not indestructible; however, it will stand up to demanding use.

Both hardwoods and softwoods are graded according to their color, grain, and imperfections.

Engineered wood, or wood-veneer flooring, consists of a thin layer of hardwood glued to layers of less-expensive plywood or pine in a process that makes them more stable than solid wood.

The light honey tones in the floor above impart a casual air, while the dark tones in the floor at right enhance the slightly more urbane vibe in this room.

Finishes

Natural wood stains range from light ash tones to deep, coffeelike colors. Generally, lighter stains make a room feel less formal, and darker, richer stains suggest a stately atmosphere. As with lighter colors, lighter stains create a feeling of openness and make a small room look larger; darker stains foster a more intimate feeling and can reduce the visual vastness of a large space.

Creative patterning of a wood floor can enrich a design. For example, create an Old World look by laying strips in a herringbone pattern. Decorative inlay with strips or parquet patterns can enhance richness and visual interest. Use inlays to "frame" areas in large open plans.

Contrasting maple strips create a low-cost focal point in the entry, left.

This 5-in.-wide engineered plank floor, opposite, has a cherry veneer stained to a deep amber color. A hand-scraped look lends "age" to this wood floor, right.

I'm planning to install a wood floor in my bedroom. What type of wood flooring is most popular?

what the experts say

"That's an impossible question to answer because it's pretty much all over the place," says Annette M. Callari, ASID, a design specialist and spokesperson for the World Floor Covering Association. "Hand-scraped wood floors offer dimensional beauty that has captivated America. And there are some new variations. But so have vintage-look floors, with all their markings and glory of years gone by. High gloss, formal dark woods still command attention and have become classic, although I see their popularity waning a bit. I would attribute that to the upkeep necessary to keep them in a state of perfection. But warm neutral gray finishes with interesting wood grains are gaining in popularity because they are so user-friendly. Across the board, I am happy to report that manufacturers have developed exciting wood finishes, glazes, and textured surfaces to replace the more exotic imported hardwoods. All of this is done in an honest endeavor to preserve rare-species forests." For more information, go to the Decorator's Corner at www.wfca.org.

A medium-tone stain strikes a perfect balance with the dark-wood furniture here.

Laminates

When your creative side tells you to install wood but your practical side knows it just won't hold up in the traffic-heavy location you're decorating, a wood floor look-alike might be just the thing. Faux-wood and faux-stone laminate floors provide you with the look you want tempered with physical wear and care properties that you and your family require. Laminate is particularly suited to rooms where floors are likely to see heavy duty—kitchens, family rooms, hallways, and children's bedrooms and playrooms—anywhere stain and scratch resistance and easy cleanup count. Prolonged exposure to moisture will damage some laminate products, but many types are treated with a water-resistant coating. Manufacturers of laminate offer warranties against staining, scratching, cracking, and peeling for up to 25 years.

This laminate flooring, above, is a dead ringer for bamboo, while the same material has been fabricated to resemble slate, below. Shown in a hickory look, opposite, laminate flooring is relatively easy to install and often quite affordable.

"Green" Flooring

Fire and moisture resistant, **cork** resists mold and comes from a sustainable resource. Some cork products are solid, while others are glued to a wood substrate. It's comfortable to stand on a cork floor, and the material is warm underfoot. Cork comes in planks, tiles, and sheeting in a variety of shades.

Bamboo is another good choice for flooring because of its durability and sustainability. It is available in two basic grain patterns, horizontal and vertical; the latter is better for damp locations. If you buy prefabricated bamboo planks, look for a low volatile-organic-compound (VOC) rating.

Cushiony horizontal-grain bamboo flooring, opposite, is a perfect choice for kitchens where people spend lots of time standing. Installed in a bedroom, engineered-bamboo flooring used with radiant heat is toasty under bare feet, right. This dining room's flooring, below right, shows the characteristic joint markings of vertical-grain bamboo.

"Green" Flooring **215**

You can create different patterns even with solid-color tile. These clay tiles, sealed to resist dirt and damage from moisture, have been installed in an interesting pattern to dress up an entry hall.

Tile and Stone

Ceramic tile and stone remain popular, especially as flooring in kitchens and baths where resistance to moisture and stains is important. Both are naturally porous, however, so make sure that the tile or stone you select is sealed (or glazed), slip resistant, and rated for use as a flooring material.

Tile is a versatile material that can pick up a decorating scheme and add color, pattern, and texture.

Refined stone tile set in a diamond pattern is an elegant choice and cool underfoot in warm climates.

These somewhat more rustic tiles resemble handmade, terra-cotta saltillo tiles.

Resilient Vinyl

Resilient flooring is available in design-friendly sheet or tile form. Price, durability, and easy maintenance make it an attractive choice.

Cushioned sheet vinyl offers the most resilience. It provides excellent stain resistance; it's comfortable and quiet underfoot; and it's easy to maintain, with no-wax and never-wax finishes often available. But only the more expensive grades show an acceptable degree of resistance to nicking and denting. Although the range of colors, patterns, and surface textures is great, sheet flooring is not as flexible as vinyl tile when it comes to customizing your floor's design.

Regular sheet vinyl is less expensive than the cushioned types, carries the same disadvantages, and is slightly less resilient. Except for the availability of no-wax finishes, a vinyl tile floor is as stain resistant and easy to maintain as the sheet-vinyl products.

Photographic reproduction and embossing combine to create the look of natural stone.

They may look like wood, left, or stone, below, but these floors are actually covered with resilient vinyl. Satin and matte finishes are popular.

Carpets and Rugs

The terms carpet and rug are often used interchangeably, but they're not the same, in terms of both manufacture and design application. Carpeting is manufactured in rolls ranging from just over 2 feet wide to broadlooms that measure as much as 18 feet wide. Carpeting is usually laid wall-to-wall and can be installed over raw subflooring. Rugs are soft floor coverings that don't extend wall-to-wall and are used over another finished-flooring surface.

Differences in fiber composition, construction, color, texture, and cost make choosing a carpet or rug a complex job. Carpeting can be made of natural wool, synthetic fibers, or blends of wool and synthetics. Other natural fibers commonly used in area rugs, scatter rugs, and mats are cotton or other plant materials such as hemp, jute, sisal, sea grass, or coir.

This pretty cotton tone-on-tone striped rug, left, features a border, above, that matches the upholstery fabric used for the stool cushions, adding a custom look. A reproduction of a vintage hand-hooked rug, opposite, pulls together the color palette in this room.

Making a Selection

Quality matters when it comes to carpeting. Wool carpeting is the most durable and the most expensive. Carpeting made from synthetic fibers offers the greatest variety in terms of color, pattern, and texture and is certainly more affordable. A good compromise choice would be a wool-synthetic blend, offering a reasonably wide variety of design options plus some enhanced durability without a pure-wool price tag.

The way a carpet or rug feels is determined by its "pile," or surface. A **loop pile** leaves loops intact when the carpet is connected to a backing. **Cut pile** has cut loops. Tip-sheared carpets are a combination of cut and uncut loops. Berber carpeting is short-loop-pile carpeting, while shag carpeting has long cut pile.

The most versatile rugs are the Orientals. Authentic, handmade versions of these rugs from the Near and Far East can be expensive, but you can find excellent, affordable reproductions. Other types of rugs include handmade dhurrie rugs from India, rya rugs from Scandinavia, and hooked, braided, and rag rugs from all parts of the globe.

Oriental rug patterns can be traditional, above, or modern. Wall-to-wall carpeting, right, is favored in a bedroom, particularly when the subfloor is unfinished.

do this... not that

good housekeeping

If allergies bother you, should you get rid of your carpet? Not necessarily. The problem may be that you are not vacuuming it often enough. (You should do it once a week.) Dust mites and other allergens can linger in the carpet's fuzzy fibers. Spot-clean your carpet as needed, and have it professionally cleaned twice a year.

How do I choose the right size and shape for an area rug?

what the experts say

According to the experts at the World Floor Covering Association, "Area rugs are made in standard and non-standard sizes, and they can be rectangular (most common), round, square, oval, octagonal, or long and narrow for runners. The most common sizes are 2 x 3 feet, 4 x 6 feet, 5 x 8 feet, 6 x 9 feet, 8 x 10 feet, and up.

"If you are thinking of a square or rectangle, place a piece of paper where each of the corners will fall in the area you wish to cover. Measure the space, and adjust the 'corners' as needed to make the space larger or smaller.

"If you're considering a round rug, run a piece of tape from the center of the space you want to cover to the outside edge. Measure it. This gives you the radius of the circle. Double it, and you have the diameter.

"Oblongs or ovals are measured as you would rectangles—by the length of the longest part and the width of the widest part. Run a measuring tape on your floor to determine the length and width of the area you want to cover."

The right-size area rug defines an intimate arrangement in front of the fireplace here.

chapter 9
living areas

The public areas of your home, the rooms in which you welcome guests, watch a movie, or gather with family at mealtimes and beyond demand a lot. They have to look and feel good, and work hard. Smart furniture choices and organization are key elements, particularly when living and family rooms are essentially the same space in open plans that incorporate "family central"—the kitchen. Here are some ideas to make these rooms special.

Cheerful colors and casually elegant furniture make this room as appealing for entertaining as it is for family time.

Welcoming Entrance Halls

This is the first view into your home, so make the entrance warm and welcoming. Because you don't spend a lot of time here, you can go bolder with color or pattern than you would in the living room, for example. But always provide a visual link to the rooms any hallway connects, perhaps using an area rug or paint to make the connection.

If space permits, a console table or a shelf is a good idea as a landing spot for keys or the mail. But avoid clutter—use a basket or a pretty bowl to contain these items until you can sort them. Add personal touches—fine art or family photographs are perfect. A mirror is practical and pretty in a foyer, and it will make a tiny hallway feel larger.

Finally, don't forget about lighting. A pendant, a chandelier, or wall sconces can add the right amount of ambient light and look decorative at the same time.

Consider entrance hall flooring carefully for style and practicality. Tile, top right, is a smart choice. Hardwood, bottom right, is handsome, but to protect its finish, use it with an area rug, opposite.

Living and Family Rooms

Today, the idea of a formal living room is almost passé. In fact, a living room is nonexistent in some new homes because it's regarded as wasted space. More often than not, people spend their leisure time at home in the family room, a more relaxed place where putting your feet up on the furniture and snacking in front of the TV is acceptable.

In a home with separate family and living rooms, the latter is typically where more formal entertaining takes place. Here is where you might splurge on fine fabrics, as opposed to the family room, which must accommodate the rough and tumble of everyday use. On the other hand, if your living room has to double as a gathering spot for casual family fare and formal entertainment, your decorating choices will have to walk the line between tasteful and hard-working.

Group seating pieces close enough for conversation but far enough from each other that people can get up and walk around or pass snacks and beverages easily.

A flat-screen TV on the wall in a family room, left, or living room, below, is fine, but hide the clutter of wires and cables inside the wall.

Just beyond the kitchen island, this home's family room is open to all the activity that is taking place in both areas.

Far right: While the kitchen is buzzing with meal preparation and clean-up, the family room provides plenty of soft seating for relaxing in front of the fire or the TV.

Top right: A large ottoman in the middle of the grouping is great for extra seating and can accommodate drink and snack trays.

Bottom right: Because the backs

it's in the
details ✱

of the upholstered pieces are visible, they are finished neatly. This is important to remember whenever furniture is not positioned against a wall.

living areas

TV and Media Rooms

All hail big flat-screen TVs and surround sound! Home theaters—rooms dedicated to watching movies and sports events—have special criteria for enjoying home entertainment in comfort. Sound and light control should be part of the plan in addition to seating that offers viewing comfort. It's a smart idea to consult a professional to design this space.

In a TV room, right, or a home theater, below, the monitor should be at least 40 inches from the seating area for comfortable viewing.

Seating designed specially for home-theater use, left, may come with built-in drink holders and a place for the remote control or a bowl of popcorn. A dedicated home theater, below, offers a crystal-clear picture and exciting surround sound. Lighting illuminating the aisles that can be dimmed for viewing is important, as are sound-proof walls.

Kitchens

The kitchen is the most popular gathering spot in the house. And while there are task-related practical considerations in terms of design, the truth is, this social hub has to be stylish and comfortable, too. Your choice of cabinets can set the style—modern, traditional, nostalgic, European country, Victorian cottage, and so forth. And your choice of finishing materials will play a part. But you'll have to make decisions about colors, light fixtures, and accents that will put together a cohesive style.

*do this... not that

you can fake it

If splurging on a granite countertop puts a dent in your budget, you can still finish your backsplash with a flourish. Ceramic tile that looks like stone is the answer. Look for a color that coordinates with the countertop. Keep the field tiles simple, and add a decorative touch here and there with accent tiles or a border.

Kitchen style starts with your cabinetry, followed by details such as light fixtures and furniture. White wood cabinets and reproduction lighting, opposite, are perfect for a Victorian-cottage look. Dark-stained wood and modern fixtures, right, define a transitional look.

A contemporary design, left, incorporates lighter cabinets into the design. A glass-tile backsplash behind the cooktop is a dramatic extra touch.

5 concrete

6 quartz

the **10**
top **10**

Surface Trends

1 **mixing materials** Combining cool metal and stone with warm wood adds depth to a design.

2 **glass** Look for this luminous material on cooktops, appliance fronts, cabinet doors, tile, and countertops.

9 engineered wood

10 stone

3 new paints They are easier to keep clean and some new types bond to all sorts of surfaces, including plastic laminate.

4 ceramic tile
- a classic choice
- lots of colors, patterns
- relatively easy to install
- many price points
- easy to maintain
- uses: floors, backsplashes, counters

5 concrete It's versatile and can be tinted, textured, and formed into interesting shapes.

6 quartz composite This nonporous, nonabsorbent surfacing material is 93 percent natural quartz; the rest is resin fillers. It is resistant to mold and mildew, scratches, stains, cracks, heat, and most household chemicals.

7 metal
- a trend that's here for the long run
- includes stainless steel and copper
- goes with any decorating style
- some finishes are fingerprint-resistant

8 solid surfacing
- durable
- many colors and patterns

- relatively easy to maintain
- sometimes available with built-in antibacterial protection
- moldable

9 engineered wood
- looks like real wood
- available in many finishes
- relatively easy to install
- easy to maintain

10 stone
- available as tiles or slabs
- many types are highly abuse-resistant
- relatively easy to maintain
- goes with any style

Indoor/Outdoor "Rooms"

Attached indoor/outdoor spaces that provide partial or total shelter can be considered extensions of the living space. When you're decorating these areas, consider all of the seasons during which you'll be using them if not year-round. And because they typically have either lots of windows or are directly exposed to sunlight, you'll want to consider fabrics and sun-control measures carefully. Over-exposure to sun and heat makes these spaces uncomfortable at certain times of the day or year and can fade textiles and wood furniture.

An enclosed porch, opposite, or a sun-room, below, offers additional living space that can be enjoyed almost year-round in some places.

Mudrooms

A practical, convenient entry at the back or side of the house, a mudroom is a buffer between indoor and outdoor life where you can remove and store everything from muddy boots to winter coats. It's also a handy spot for storing sports gear, backpacks, and lunch boxes. Organization is key, so make sure to outfit your mudroom with hooks and cubbies that will contain all of these things. Sometimes the laundry is incorporated in a mudroom. In that case, try to include space for separating, folding, and ironing clothes.

Built-in cubbies and racks, left, keep an entire family's assortment of hats, backpacks, sneakers, and more neatly contained. A back hall, above, shares laundry space with a rack for coats and even the dog's leash, above. Cabinets store sports equipment, right. A tile floor is easy to clean after muddy boots track dirt inside.

chapter 10
bed and bath

The private areas of a home, specifically bedrooms and bathrooms, deserve the royal treatment. After all, they are intended for someone important—you. Tailor them to your needs. Create havens where you can tune out the world, relax, and recharge. Choose restful colors, and address privacy and light control with suitable window treatments. In addition, look for ways to keep clutter at bay. Whether it's you, your children, or a guest who will use this space, make it comfortable, convenient, and personal.

244

A few luxurious touches make this bedroom the perfect retreat for quiet personal time.

Master Suites

Few places offer the privacy and quiet of a bedroom, and these are the qualities that make it an ideal personal retreat. Resist the temptation to make this a multipurpose room. It's not the place for the computer or the home office, and taking work into the bedroom is not a restful concept.

Start with a feeling—the sense you get when you are in a calm, restful environment. Try to create this ambiance through your choice of colors, textures, furniture, and accessories. Use color and theme to create a link between the master bedroom and bath. Special amenities, such as spa features, can add to your comfort and make the master suite truly a place to get away from it all.

Earth tones keep the mood in this master bedroom and its en suite bath restful. The colors of nature are soothing, and so they are a perfect choice for a part of the home that is meant for decompressing. The palette is particularly successful in the spa-inspired bath, top and opposite.

A daybed is a versatile choice for girls or boys, especially when it comes with a trundle or pop-up mattress that can accommodate sleepovers.

Kids' Bedrooms

Playful, happy themes can create fun rooms for kids, but resist the temptation to make the space too juvenile. Look for furniture and decorating themes that can last from young childhood through teen years, with perhaps a little tweaking along the way. It's a good idea to avoid movie- and toy-inspired themes that quickly go in and out of fashion. Even when the room is small, you can find ways to contain kid stuff using colorful bins and baskets. Install a closet organizing system to stretch space, and don't forget about wall shelves for display and storage.

Simple window treatments that can be easily opened or closed, but without dangerous cords, are perfect for young kids' rooms.

Nursery

Fortunately, the absolute furniture necessities for a nursery are few. Start with the basics—a crib; a changing table; a comfortable chair, rocker, or glider; a chest of drawers and side table; and lighting. You can fill in later with those items you discover will make it easier and more comfortable for you to care for your baby. Buying versatile furniture that can serve different roles at various times during your child's development is a clever investment. A crib that converts to a junior bed and a changing table with drawers that offer storage space are a couple of options.

Your baby isn't going to notice too much about his or her room's decor, but you might want to coordinate it with the rest of your home. Bright green fabric blinds are cheerful in this room, left. Touches of bright red, above, in solid, plaid, and toile fabrics will be suitable for years to come.

Safety in the Nursery

It's not difficult to make your newborn's room a safe environment. After all, a baby spends most of his time either in the crib or in your arms. But babies grow fast, becoming more independent with each day. Because your child will be a busy toddler before you know it, you may want to think ahead and get the room ready for the age of exploration. Here's a checklist that will help you childproof the room for a young baby.

- Install outlet caps and covers on all electrical outlets.
- Play it safe with electrical cords. Don't run them under the carpet, and don't let them dangle from a tabletop or dresser.
- Use only blinds and shades without looped cords.
- Your baby's ability to pull herself up on the crib rails will likely coincide with her teething schedule. To protect her from swallowing paint or varnish chips, install snap-on crib rail protectors.
- Install childproof locks on drawers and cabinets.
- Tack down carpets.
- Keep the crib far enough away from any window so that the baby can't grab any cords or curtains or try to climb out the window.
- Remove small objects and toys with small parts that the baby might swallow.
- Make sure furniture is assembled properly. Check for loose nuts and bolts.
- Hang a mobile out of the reach of the baby. Once the baby can stand, remove the mobile to ensure his safety.
- Keep the side rails up at all times when the baby is in the crib.
- Install a smoke alarm in the room.
- Use a monitor to listen to the baby when you're away from the room.
- Follow the recommendations of the Consumer Product Safety Commission regarding cribs.

From Tween to Teen

Not babies but still kids, this age group shares some common needs. By this time, children want to be involved in decisions concerning their rooms. You can provide comfortable furnishings, storage amenities, and a space for a computer and studying. But they'll want to take the lead regarding color choices and in choosing the personal touches and accessories that express their point of view.

do this... not that

"window" shopping

You may not be able to drag your tween or teen to a furniture store or to shop with you for linens, but you can get an idea about what they like by shopping the new-fashioned way—online. The experience isn't quite the same as in-person shopping, but depending on the site, you will get a lot of ideas that you can discuss.

A boy's interest in the sea and sailing inspired this wall mural, opposite top. An attractive, comfortable work area, left, helps kids focus on studies. A young artist's love of color finds expression in her choice of wall paint and textiles, below.

Guest Rooms

Give guests a thoughtful place of their own to sleep, work, or just relax alone. Start with a quality bed, mattress, pillows, and linens. Give special thought to furnishing the room with storage pieces, such as a chest of drawers. And don't forget about function. A desk for working at their laptop, a comfortable chair for lounging, a radio (or a TV), and magazines will make them feel at home. So will closet space, even if it's not an entire closet. Stock a basket with small amenities, too: a toothbrush, shampoos, nice soaps, and fresh towels. Keep clutter to a minimum so that the room feels and looks fresh.

A pretty room of their own tells your guests that they are welcome. A comfortable bed dressed in beautiful linens, above, is a thoughtful gesture. This room also has an adjacent bath, opposite.

Today's Bath Trends

Today's bathrooms are designed to pamper, whether the actual layout is large or small. Good-looking materials and finishes make it possible to add glamour, but not at the expense of function thanks to the sophisticated technology used in the latest bath and shower fixtures. When a bath is en suite, coordinate color motifs. The same or similar style and finish for bathroom cabinetry and bedroom furniture provides another link, as do lighting fixtures and hardware.

Water tiles built into the
walk-in shower's wall,
right, are strategically
located and can be aimed
at any tired muscle.

A built-in dresser, opposite far left,
makes practical use of a small nook in
this design. When privacy isn't an issue,
bringing nature into the bath, left, is a
luxury that everyone can afford.

STEP 1 analyze your needs

Make a list of who will use the new bathroom and how much storage they need. Besides clean towels, will you need a place for rolls of tissue, grooming and cleaning supplies, and small appliances?

If young children will use the room, plan a place to store bath toys—not on the floor where someone can trip on them. If they will be sharing the bath with adults, include a cabinet that can be locked, unless you can safely store medicines and other potentially harmful substances where children can't get access to them. Never store medicine on an open shelf.

STEP 2 divide and conquer

Make a plan now to store similar items, such as all bath towels on one shelf, all hand towels on another shelf. Keep grooming products and cosmetics together and separate from bathroom cleaners.

■ **Niches.** One way to stretch the storage capacity and compartmentalize it in a bathroom is to create recessed niches between the studs inside the walls. Locate them in different points of use, such as in the wall of the shower for shampoos, soaps, and shaving creams. Install another one near the toilet for an extra roll or two of tissue, or create one long niche for towels and a hamper.

STEP 3 accessorize

Some of the interior options offered for kitchen cabinets are available for bathroom vanities. Slide-out trays and lazy Susans, for example, make it easy to find items that are stored in the back of the cabinet, and you can corral laundry in a rollout bin. There are racks for everything from hairbrushes and curling irons to bulky blow dryers that you can mount to the inside of cabinet doors.

If you are ordering custom or semicustom cabinetry for your bathroom, you can also ask for compartmentalized drawers that can separate items such as cotton swabs and bobby pins from one another.

STEP 4 multiply

The vanity still reigns as the major supplier of storage in the bathroom. Because one height does not suit all, stock vanities now range from the standard 30 inches to 36 inches high. With two vanities in a shared bath, each one can be tailored to a comfortable height for its user. Shallow 18-inch-deep units free up floor space while 24-inch-deep models store more.

If you have the space, consider installing additional cabinetry in the bathroom. If you don't want to go the custom route, you can find coordinated suites of stock cabinetry from the major manufacturers.

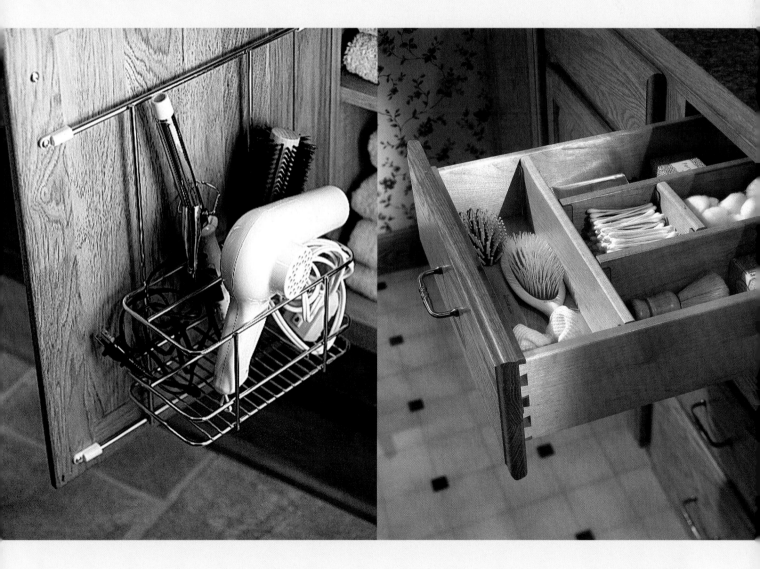

Powder Rooms

A pretty powder room is easy to pull together, even when you're on a tight budget. Typically small, it doesn't require all that much to make it more than utilitarian and impress your guests. And you don't have to be overly concerned about exposing a delicate wallcovering to water damage and mold, either. Don't be afraid to go bold with color and pattern despite the small size of the room. Here's your chance to go over the top.

go green

NATURAL BEAUTY

When you're looking for a vanity, check out cabinets that have been manufactured in an environmentally responsible manner. Use wood certified and labeled by the Forestry Stewardship Council (FSC); visit www.fscus.org. Or retrofit an old chest with a plumbing system. Apply deck sealer to protect its finish.

The tile and vessel lav bring an exotic look into this powder room, opposite. Damask wallpaper and white paneling, left, tie this room to the home's traditional style. An antique chest of drawers, plumbed and fitted with a marble countertop and under-mounted sink, serves as a unique piece in this half bath, above.

3 use corners

4 round it out

the 10
top 10
Half-Bath Tips

1 color Even if you feel timid about using deep colors elsewhere, go for it here. Kick it up a notch with
◆ a glossy finish
◆ texture

2 pattern Bold pattern in a tiny room? Absolutely! Use oversize wallpaper and fabric patterns. Large prints make big statements, and your powder room will look grand.

3 use corners and angles Angle a vanity in a corner. Install corner fixtures.

4 round it out Curved or round furnishings take the boxy look out of a small space.

5 nip and tuck Extend a portion of the vanity counter over a toilet tank.

8 go for glamour

5 nip and tuck

10 pamper your guests

6 install a pedestal sink A pedestal sink is pretty, and it makes good use of small space.

7 include good lighting It's important to install proper lighting in every bathroom. Remember, your guests may be using the powder room to touch up makeup.

8 go for glamour Splurge on special fixtures: a small chandelier, a handpainted lav, or gorgeous fittings.

9 use an antique Swap a standard vanity, and retrofit an antique table, cabinet, or chest with a lav and faucet. This is a great way to create a unique style statement—and you can sometimes find a bargain piece at a flea market or garage sale.

10 pamper your guests Include special hand towels, soaps, and lotions. Fresh flowers are always a beautiful touch.

Kids' Baths

You may want to address some special issues in a bathroom designed for young children. Safety is always a concern, so install countertops or sinks that suit the height of the children who will use the room. If you don't want to have to replace these items later, build a step into the vanity's toe-kick area to give little ones a boost. Function-wise, install a handheld sprayer in the shower at a height that is easy for your youngsters to reach. Lever valves are also more comfortable than faucets that have knobs or handles.

A small handheld sprayer is easy for little hands to grasp and is located at a suitable height on the shower wall, below. At the vanity, opposite, there's room for two kids to groom. A small stool tucked under the counter is there for a boost.

A shared bath, above, accommodates everyone, with separate lavs and mirrors scaled for big and little kids.

appendix

window and door templates

Windows

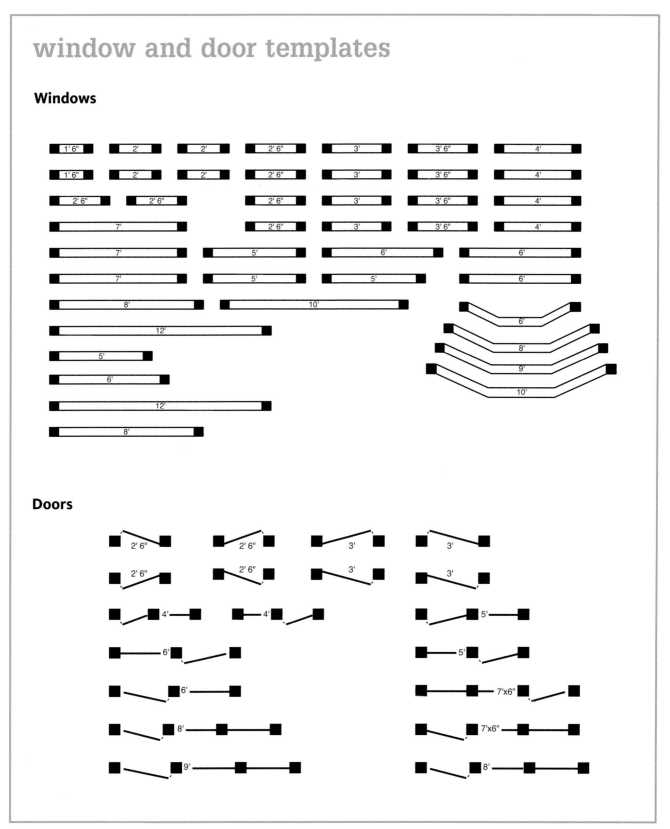

Doors

furniture templates

Sofas, Love Seats, and Sofa Beds

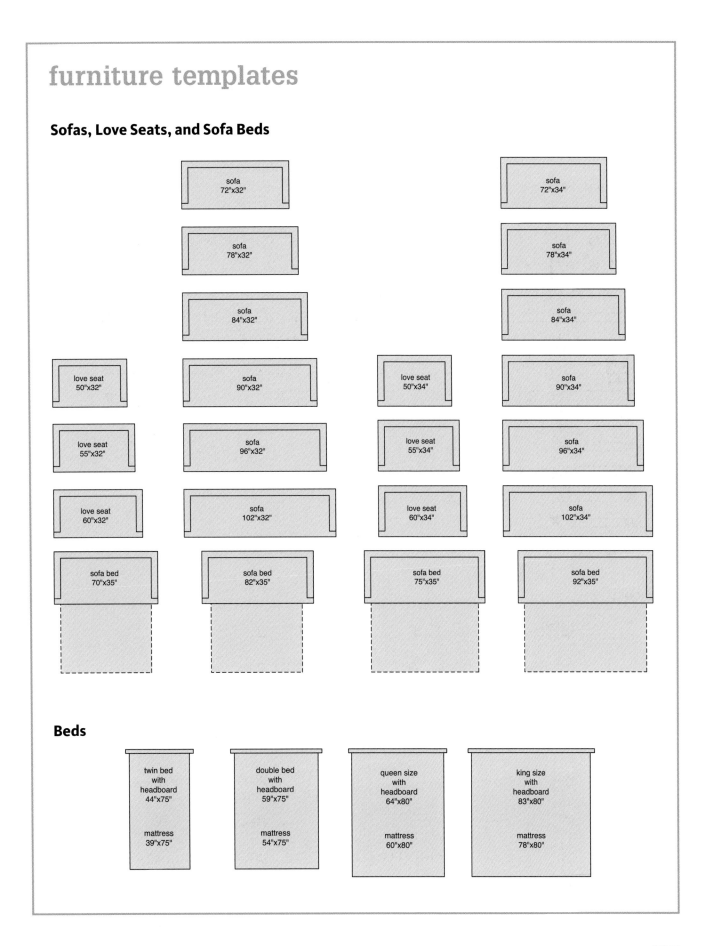

sofa
72"x32"

sofa
72"x34"

sofa
78"x32"

sofa
78"x34"

sofa
84"x32"

sofa
84"x34"

love seat
50"x32"

sofa
90"x32"

love seat
50"x34"

sofa
90"x34"

love seat
55"x32"

sofa
96"x32"

love seat
55"x34"

sofa
96"x34"

love seat
60"x32"

sofa
102"x32"

love seat
60"x34"

sofa
102"x34"

sofa bed
70"x35"

sofa bed
82"x35"

sofa bed
75"x35"

sofa bed
92"x35"

Beds

twin bed
with
headboard
44"x75"

mattress
39"x75"

double bed
with
headboard
59"x75"

mattress
54"x75"

queen size
with
headboard
64"x80"

mattress
60"x80"

king size
with
headboard
83"x80"

mattress
78"x80"

furniture templates

Chairs and Ottomans

left-arm module 32"x32"

armless module 32"x32"

right-arm module 32"x32"

ottoman 32"x32"

wing chair 33"x34"

lounge chair 32"x32"

lounge chair 30"x30"

barrel chair 30"x30"

headrest

barrel chair 30"x29" (opens to 66") footrest

rocking chair 22"x24"

arm-chair 27"x29"

arm-chair 27"x27"

occasional chair 23"x26"

occasional chair 25"x25"

occasional chair 24"x22"

ottoman 30"x16"

ottoman 27"x20"

ottoman 22"x22"

chaise longue 60"x24"

32" round ottoman

End Tables

square table 36"x36"

square table 28"x28"

square table 27"x27"

square table 20"x20"

square table 18"x18"

square table 16"x16"

end table 14"x20"

end table 16"x22"

end table 22"x26"

end table 22"x28"

end table 18"x28"

end table 20"x24"

end table 21"x30"

end table 16"x25"

end table 16"x27"

end table 18"x24"

Coffee Tables and Desks

18" round table

24" round table

console 40"x20"

nest of tables 24"x16"

20"x 29"x29"

28"x 28"x28"

desk 60"x30"

table 66"x20"

table 60"x20"

table 44"x22"

desk 50"x25"

table 54"x22"

table 60"x22"

table 70"x22"

desk 40"x18"

table 58"x24"

table 66"x28"

table 66"x32"

corner desk 32"x32"

furniture templates

Accessories

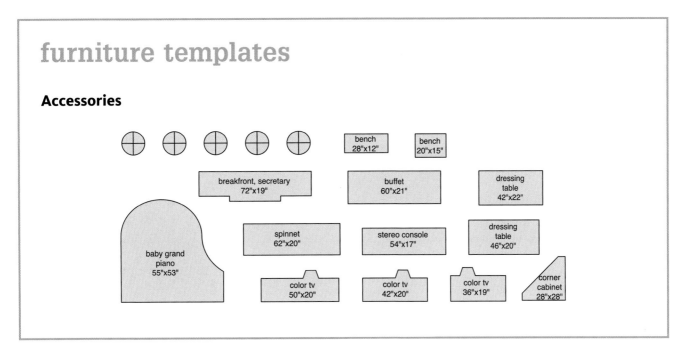

kitchen templates

Dining and Café Tables

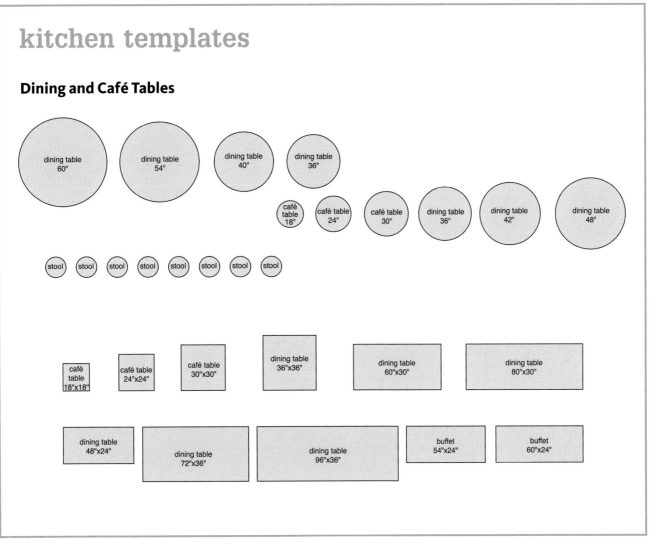

kitchen templates

Countertops

Base Cabinets

Islands and Appliances

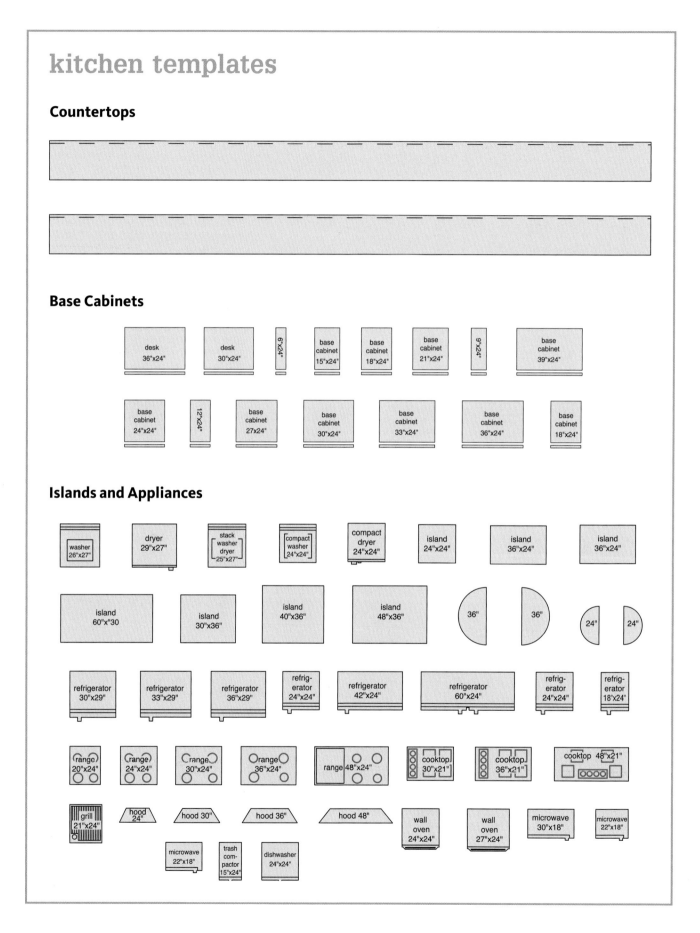

kitchen templates

Sinks

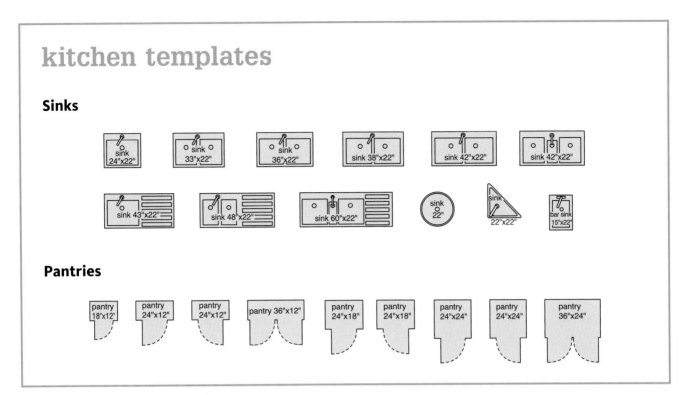

Pantries

bathroom templates

Lavatories

Toilets

Tubs and Shower

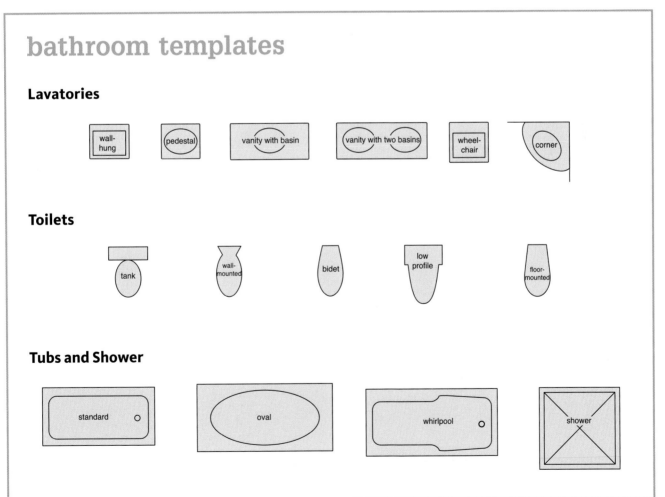

Scale: 1 square=1 foot

resource guide

The following list of manufacturers and associations is meant to be a general guide to additional industry and product-related sources. It is not intended as a listing of products and manufacturers represented by the photographs in this book.

MANUFACTURERS

Ballard Designs
800-536-7551
www.ballarddesigns.com
Sells furniture, accessories, wall decor, tableware, rugs, and lighting.

Benjamin Moore & Co.
www.benjaminmoore.com
Manufactures paint.

Century Furniture
800-852-5552
www.centuryfurniture.com
Manufactures furniture for both indoors and outdoors.

Comfortex Window Fashions
800-843-4151
www.comfortex.com
Manufactures custom window treatments, including sheer and pleated shades, wood shutters, and blinds.

Country Curtains
800-937-1237
www.countrycurtains.com
A national retailer and online source for ready-made curtains, shades, blinds, hardware, and accessories.

Crate & Barrel
800-967-6696
www.crateandbarrel.com
A national retailer and online source for furniture, decorating items and ideas, and accessories.

Drexel Heritage
www.drexelheritage.com
Manufactures furniture.

Ethan Allen Furniture
888-324-3571
www.ethanallen.com
Manufactures upholstered furniture and casegoods.

Fabric Workroom
800-377-9182
www.fabricworkroom.com
Manufactures custom window treatments, pillows, and bedding.

Furniture Quest
www.furniturequest.com
Provides sources for furniture home decor.

Glidden
800-454-3336
www.glidden.com
Manufactures paint.

Graber Window Fashions
Spring Industries
888-926-7888
www.springs.com
Manufacturers blinds and shades.

Home Decorators Collection
877-537-8539
www.homedecorators.com
Sells furniture, lighting, and storage systems.

IKEA
217-347-7701
www.ikea.com
Manufactures and sells home furnishings, kitchen appliances, cabinets, sinks, faucets, and countertops.

Karastan
800-234-1120
www.karastan.com
Manufactures and sells rugs and carpets.

Kathryn Ireland
310-837-8890
www.kathrynireland.com
Manufactures textiles, bedding, lighting, and furniture.

Kohler
800-456-4537
www.kohlerco.com
Manufactures kitchen and bath sinks, faucets, and related accessories.

KraftMaid Cabinetry
888-562-7744
www.kraftmaid.com
Manufactures stock and built-to-order cabinets with a variety of finishes and storage options.

Kravet
516-293-2000
www.kravet.com
Manufactures fabrics and ready-made furnishings.

Lamps USA
877-526-7247
www.lampsusa.com
Manufactures lighting fixtures.

Lane Furniture
www.lanefurniture.com
Manufactures home furnishings.

Layla Grace
877-907-1322
www.laylagrace.com
Sells a boutique collection of nursery furnishings.

Lightology
866-954-4489
www.lightology.com
Manufactures lighting fixtures.

My Perfect Color
888-307-1729
www.myperfectcolor.com
Provides an online guide to color and color combinations, as well as inspirational ideas.

The Nantucket BeadBoard Company Inc.
603-330-1070
www.beadboard.com
Manufactures beadboard in a variety of profiles.

North Carolina Furniture and Mattress
800-913-9138
www.ncfurniture.com
Sells discounted furniture and mattresses.

North Carolina Furniture Directory
www.highpointfurniture.com
Provide a list of furniture manufacturers and outlets in North Carolina.

Paint Quality Institute
www.paintquality.com
Provides information on paint selection and painting.

Pantone
866-726-8663
www.pantone.com
Provides color systems and guides.

Pottery Barn
888-779-5176
www.potterybarn.com
Sells home furnishings in stores nationwide and online.

Raymour and Flanigan
866-383-4484
www.raymourflanigan.com
Retails home furnshings nationwide.

Restoration Hardware
800-910-9836
www.restorationhardware.com
Sells its line of home furnishings in stores nationwide and online.

Seagrass Furniture

310-324-8101

www.seagrass-furniture.com

Manufactures natural woven sofas, chairs, tables, and accessories.

Sherwin-Williams

800-474-3794

www.sherwin-williams.com

Manufactures paint.

Sofa-Guide

www.sofa-guide.com

Provides in-depth information on purchasing and maintaining a sofa.

Stickley Furniture

315-682-5500

www.stickley.com

Manufactures solid-wood furniture.

The Shade Store

800-754-1455

www.theshadestore.com

Manufactures custom window treatments.

Thibaut Inc.

800-223-0704

www.thibautdesign.com

Manufactures wallpaper and fabrics.

Thomasville Furniture Industries

www.thomasville.com

Manufactures furniture.

Wood-Mode Fine Custom Cabinetry

877-635-7500

www.wood-mode.com

Manufactures semicustom and custom cabinetry.

York Wallcoverings

717-846-4456

www.yorkwall.com

Manufactures wallpaper and borders.

ASSOCIATIONS

American Coatings Association (ACA)

202-462-6272

www.paint.org

A nonprofit trade association offering consumer information.

American Institute for Conservation of Historic and Artistic Works

202-452-9545

www.conservation-us.org

Provides information on restoring and maintaining antiques.

American Society of Interior Designers (ASID)

202-546-3480

www.asid.org

A professional organization of interior designers offering referral services to consumers.

National Association of Remodeling Industry (NARI)

847-298-9200

www.nari.org

A professional organization for remodelers, contractors, and design/remodelers; also offers consumer information.

National Kitchen and Bath Association (NKBA)

800-843-6522

www.nkba.org

A national trade organization for kitchen and bath design professionals; offers consumers product information and a referral service.

World Floor Covering Association (WFCA)

800-843-6522

www.wfca.org

Dedicated to providing consumers the service and support needed to ensure a successful floor covering purchase experience.

glossary

Accent Lighting: A type of directional lighting that highlights an area or object to emphasize that aspect of a room's character.

Accessible Designs: Designs that accommodate persons with physical disabilities.

Adaptable Designs: Designs that can be easily changed to accommodate a person with disabilities.

Analogous Scheme: See Harmonious Color Scheme.

Ambient Lighting: General illumination that surrounds a room and is not directional.

Art Deco: A decorative style that was based on geometric forms. It was popular during the 1920s and 1930s.

Art Nouveau: A late-nineteenth-century decorative style that was based on natural forms. It was the first style to reject historical references and create its own design vocabulary, which was ornamental and included stylized curved details.

Arts and Crafts: An architectural and decorative style that began in England during the late nineteenth century, where it was known as the Aesthetic Movement. Lead by William Morris, the movement rejected industrialization and encouraged fine craftsmanship and simplicity in design.

Backlighting: Illumination coming from a source behind or at the side of an object.

Backsplash: The vertical part at the rear and sides of a countertop that protects the adjacent wall.

Box Pleat: A double pleat, underneath which the edges fold toward each other.

Broadloom: A wide loom for weaving carpeting that is 54 inches wide or more.

Built-in: Any element, such as a bookcase or cabinetry, that is built into a wall or an existing frame.

Cabriole: A double-curve or reverse S-shaped furniture leg that leads down to an elaborate foot (usually a ball-and-claw type).

Casegoods: A piece of furniture used for storage, including cabinets, dressers, and desks.

Clearance: The amount of space between two fixtures, the centerlines of two fixtures, or a fixture and an obstacle, such as a wall.

Code: A locally or nationally enforced mandate regarding structural design, materials, plumbing, or electrical systems that state what you can or cannot do when you build or remodel.

Color Wheel: A diagram, usually circular, showing the range and relationships of pigment and dye colors.

Complementary Colors: Hues directly opposite each other on the color wheel. As the strongest contrasts, complements tend to intensify each other.

Contemporary: Any modern design (after 1920) that does not contain traditional elements.

Dimmer Switch: A switch that can vary the intensity of the light it controls.

Faux Finish: A decorative paint technique that imitates a pattern found in nature.

Federal: An architectural and decorative style popular in America during the early nineteenth century, featuring delicate ornamentation, often depicting swags and urns, and symmetrically arranged rooms.

Fittings: The plumbing devices such as faucets that bring water to the fixtures.

Focal Point: The dominant element in a room or design, usually the first to catch your eye.

Framed Cabinet: A cabinet with a full frame across the face of the cabinet box.

Frameless Cabinet: A cabinet without a face frame. It may also be called a "European-style" cabinet.

Frieze: A horizontal band at the top of the wall or just below the cornice.

Full-Spectrum Light: Light that contains the full range of wavelengths that can be found in daylight, including invisible radiation (ultraviolet and infrared) at each end of the visible spectrum.

Georgian: An architectural and decorative style popular during the late eighteenth century, with rooms characterized by the use of paneling and other woodwork, and bold colors.

Gothic Revival: An architectural and decorative style popular during the mid-nineteenth century. It romanticized the design vocabulary of the medieval period, using elements such as pointed arches and trefoils (three-leaf motifs).

Greek Revival: An architectural and decorative style that drew inspiration from ancient Greek designs. It is characterized by the use of pediments and columns.

Harmonious Color Scheme: Also called analogous, a combination focused on neighboring hues on the color wheel. The shared underlying color generally gives such schemes a coherent flow.

Hue: Another term for specific points on the pure, clear range of the color wheel.

Indirect lighting: A subdued type of lighting that is not head-on, but rather reflected against another surface such as a ceiling.

Inlay: A decoration, usually consisting of stained wood, metal, or mother-of-pearl, that is set into the surface of an object in a pattern and finished flush.

Lumen: The measurement of a source's light output—the quantity of visible light.

Molding: An architectural band used to cover the line where materials join or to create a linear decoration. It is typically made of wood, plaster, or a polymer.

Neoclassic: Any revival of the ancient styles of Greece and Rome, particularly during the late eighteenth and early nineteenth centuries.

Panel: A flat, rectangular piece of material that forms part of a wall, door, or cabinet. Typically made of wood, it is usually framed by a border and either raised or recessed.

Pattern Matching: To align a repeating pattern when joining together two pieces of fabric or wallpaper.

Pediment: A triangular piece found over doors, windows, and mantles. It also refers to a low-pitched gable on the front of a building.

Peninsula: A countertop, with or without a base cabinet, that is connected at one end to a wall or another counter and extends outward, providing access on three sides.

Primary Color: Red, blue, or yellow that can't be produced in pigments by mixing other colors. Primaries plus black and white, in turn, combine to make all the other hues.

Secondary Color: A mix of two primaries. The secondary colors are orange, green, and purple.

Task lighting: Directional lighting that concentrates in specific areas for tasks, such as preparing food, applying makeup, reading, or doing crafts.

Tone: Degree of lightness or darkness of a color.

Track Lighting: Lighting that utilizes a fixed band that supplies a current to movable light fixtures.

Trompe l'oeil: French for "fool the eye"; a painted mural in which realistic images and the illusion of three-dimensional space are created.

Tufting: The fabric of an upholstered piece or a mattress that is drawn tightly to secure the padding, creating regularly spaced indentations.

index

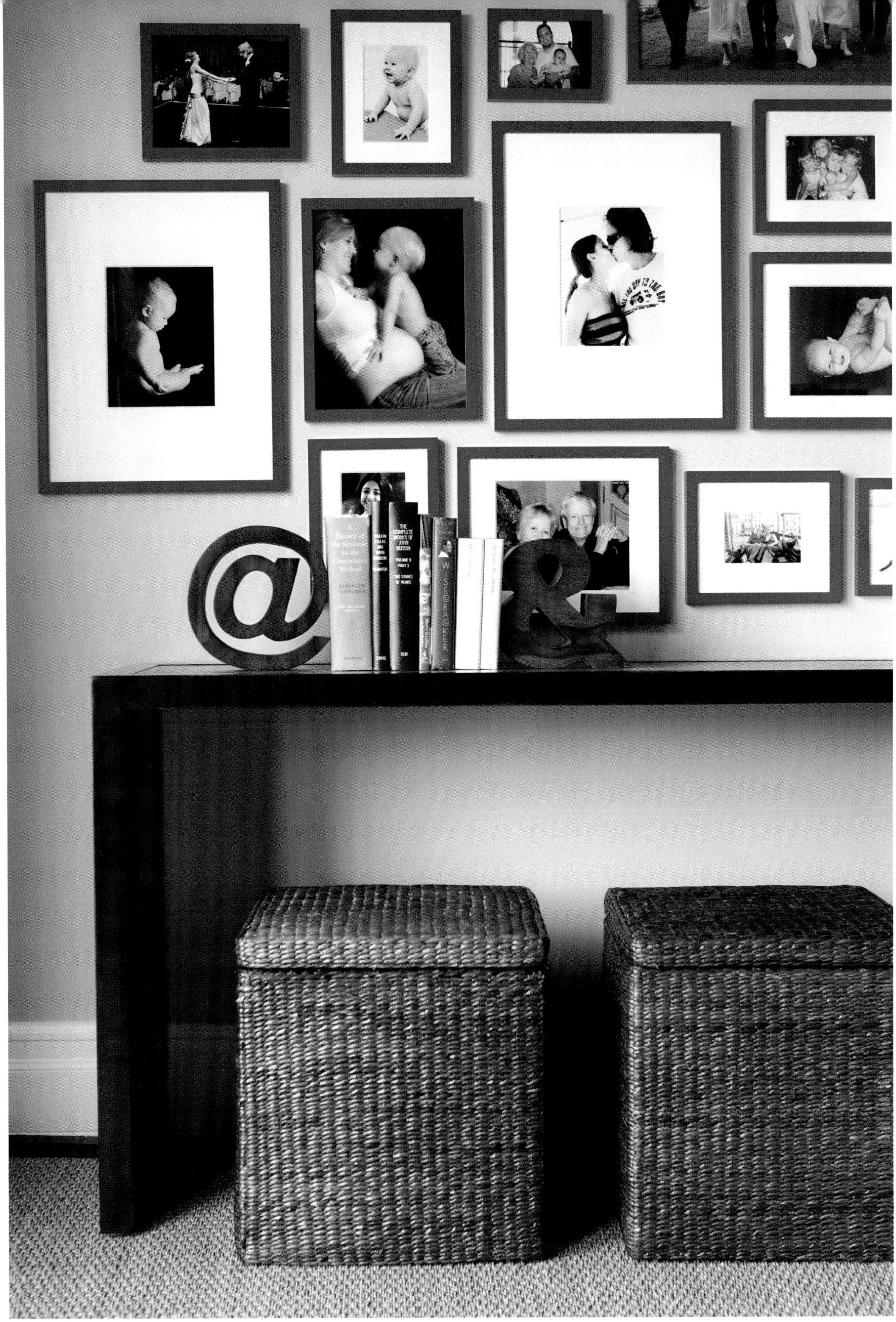

photo credits

page 1: Karyn R. Millet page 2: Karyn R. Millet, design: Bonesteel Trout Hall pages 5–9: all Mark Lohman, design: Barclay Butera Inc. pages 10–11: Eric Roth, builder: Orr Builders pages 12–13: both Tria Giovan, design: Phillip Sides page 14: Eric Roth, design/builder: jwconstruction-inc.com page 15: Photoshot/Red Cover/Robin Stubbert pages 16–17: Eric Roth, design: weenaandspook.com pages 18–19: all Eric Roth page 20: Bob Greenspan, stylist: Susan Andrews page 21: Eric Roth pages 22–23: all Mark Samu, design: Eileen Boyd Interiors pages 24–25: all Karyn R. Millet, design: Katrin Cargill & Carol Glasser pages 26–27: Stacy Bass, design: Shelley Morris Interior Design LTD pages 28–29: all Mark Lohman, design: Barclay Butera Inc. page 30: both Tria Giovan, design: Keller Donovan page 31: Bob Greenspan, stylist: Susan Andrews page 32: Tony Giammarino/Giammarino & Dworkin page 33: top Susan Gilmore; bottom Tria Giovan, design: Keller Donovan pages 34–35: all Bob Greenspan, stylist: Susan Andrews pages 36–37: Eric Roth, design: matthewsapera.com pages 38–39: Mark Lohman, design: Barclay Butera Inc. page 40: Karyn R. Millet, design: Bonesteel Trout Hall page 41: top Roy Inman, stylist: Susan Andrews; bottom Stacy Bass pages 42–43: left Mark Lohman; right Eric Roth, design: John DeBastiani page 44: left Stacy Bass, design: Patricia Lynch Design; right Karyn R. Millet, design: Tim Barber Ltd page 45: Olson Photographic, LLC, design: StaceyGendelmanDesigns.com page 46: top Susan Gilmore, design: David Heide Design, DHDStudio.com; bottom Tony Giammarino/Giammarino & Dworkin page 47: Tony Giammarino/Giammarino & Dworkin, design: Tom Duke of Evolve pages 48–49: all Tria Giovan, design: Laurann Claridge pages 50–51: Eric Roth page 52: melabee m miller, design: Nancee Brown, ASID page 53: Tony Giammarino/Giammarino & Dworkin page 55: Eric Roth, design: susansargent.com pages 56–57: left Eric Roth; right Mark Samu page 58: Eric Roth, builder: Columbia Builders page 59: Karyn R.

Millet, design: by Carrie Cusack pages 60–61: both Eric Roth pages 62–63: left Karyn R. Millet, architect: Scott Joyce; right melabee m miller, design: Nancee Brown, ASID pages 64–65: all Mark Lohman page 66: Eric Roth, design: johndd.com pages 67–68: all melabee m miller, design: Nancee Brown, ASID page 69: Tony Giammarino/Giammarino & Dworkin, design: DialMyersDesign.com pages 70–71: left Tony Giammarino/Giammarino & Dworkin, design: GwaltneyFleming.com; right Ken Hayden/Red Cover/Photoshot page 72: Robin Stubbert/Red Cover/Photoshot, design: Herma Vegter-Petrie page 73: top Robin Stubbert/Red Cover/Photoshot; bottom Red Cover/Home Journal/Photoshot pages 74–75: both Mark Samu page 76: Olson Photographic, LLC, design/builder: VAS Construction page 77: Mark Samu, design: Lucianna Samu Design pages 78–79: all Karyn R. Millet, design: Carrie Cusack pages 80–81: all Mark Lohman, design: Barclay Butera Inc. page 82: courtesy of Thibaut Inc. page 83: left courtesy of Thibaut Inc.; right Bob Greenspan, stylist: Susan Andrews page 84: Karyn R. Millet, design: Bonesteel Trout Hall page 85: courtesy of Thibaut Inc. page 86: left courtesy of Thibaut Inc.; right Karyn R. Millet, design: Jessica Brende page 87: Eric Roth, design: susansargent.com pages 88–89: left Karyn R. Millet, design: Melrose Project; middle Ken Hayden/Red Cover/Photoshot; right courtesy of Thibaut Inc. page 90: left Tony Giammarino/Giammarino & Dworkin; right Eric Roth, design: weenaandspook.com page 91: Susan Gilmore, design: Martha O'Hara Interiors, oharainteriors.com pages 92–93: Karyn R. Millet, design: Peter Fisher, architect: William F. Holland page 94: Stacy Bass page 95: left Karyn R. Millet; right Eric Roth pages 96–97: top left Mark Lohman, design: Barclay Butera Inc.; top right Bob Greenspan, stylist: Susan Andrews; bottom Tony Giammarino/Giammarino & Dworkin, design: CESpitzer.com pages 98–99: all Mark Lohman, design: Janet Lohman Interior Design pages 100–101: all Eric Roth, design: weenaandspook.com pages 102–103: all Karyn R.

Millet, design: Bonesteel Trout Hall pages 104–105: both Bob Greenspan, stylist: Susan Andrews page 106: Karyn R. Millet, design: Joan Behnke page 107: Eric Roth, design: Anamika Design pages 108–109: Eric Roth pages 110–111: all Mark Lohman, design: Barclay Butera Inc. pages 112–113: all Tony Giammarino/Giammarino & Dworkin; bottom right design: CorySpencer.com page 114: both Karyn R. Millet; left design: Chad Eisner; right design: Michael Fullen, M@ Design page 115: left Bob Greenspan, stylist: Susan Andrews; right Karyn R. Millet, design: Carrie Cusack pages 116–117: Karyn R. Millet page 118: Karyn R. Millet, design: Katrin Cargill & Carol Glasser page 119: top Tria Giovan; bottom Olson Photographic, LLC page 120: melabee m miller, design: Deck House, LLC page 121: top left Roy Inman, stylist: Susan Andrews; top right Mark Lohman; bottom right Olson Photographic, LLC, design: InnerSpace Electronics page 122: melabee m miller, design: Nancee Brown, ASID page 123: Karyn R. Millet page 124: left Eric Roth; right Andrew Wood/Red Cover/Photoshot page 125: left melabee m miller, design: Tammy Kaplan, Images in Design; right Tony Giammarino/Giammarino & Dworkin, design: Frankie Slaughter page 126: top melabee m miller, design: Nancee Brown, ASID; bottom Mark Samu page 127: Mark Lohman page 128: Olson Photographic, LLC, design: Country Club Homes page 129: melabee m miller, design: Arlene Reilly/Bernards Decorating Inc. page 130: both Karyn R. Millet, design: Bonesteel Trout Hall page 131: melabee m miller, design: Nancee Brown, ASID pages 132–133: Tony Giammarino/Giammarino & Dworkin page 134: Eric Roth page 135: Tony Giammarino/Giammarino & Dworkin, design: Jenny Andrews Designs pages 136–137: left Tony Giammarino/Giammarino & Dworkin, design: Frankie Slaughter; middle all Frank Dyer; top right melabee m miller, design: Nancee Brown, ASID; bottom right Karyn R. Millet pages 138–139: all Karyn R. Miller page 140: melabee m miller, design: Pat Mills/Byford & Mills page 141: top Mark

Lohman, design: Barclay Butera Inc.; *bottom* Susan Gilmore, design: Martha O'Hara Interiors, oharainteriors.com **page 142:** Olson Photographic, LLC **page 143:** *top* Bob Greenspan, stylist: Susan Andrews; *bottom* Mark Lohman **pages 144–145:** Tria Giovan, design: Katie Stassi **page 146:** *top* melabee m miller, design: Nancee Brown, ASID; *bottom* Olson Photographic, LLC, architect: Terry Architecture **pages 147–149:** *all* melabee m miller, design: Nancee Brown, ASID **pages 150–151:** *all* melabee m miller, design: Nancee Brown, ASID *except middle* design: Diane Romanowski **page 152:** *all* melabee m miller; *top left* design: Barbara Noud/Allied Member ASID, Lifestyle Interiors; *top right* design: James Greener, AIA & Judy Mashburn/James Greener, AIA/CTS Group; *bottom* design: Nancee Brown, ASID **page 153:** *all* melabee m miller; *top both* design: Nancee Brown, ASID; *bottom* design: Suzanne Curtis, ASID **pages 154–155:** Mark Lohman, design: Barclay Butera Inc. **pages 156–157:** Karyn R. Millet, design: Bonesteel Trout Hall **page 158:** Eric Roth, design: charlesspada.com **page 159:** *left* Stacy Bass, design: Shelley Morris Interior Design LTD; *right* Eric Roth, design: christofiinteriors.com **pages 160–161:** *left* Karyn R. Millet; *center* Tony Giammarino/Giammarino & Dworkin, design: Nita Enoch Interiors; *right* Karyn R. Millet **page 162:** *top* Stacy Bass, design: Yvonne Claveloux; bottom Sandra Cunningham/Dreamstime.com **page 163:** Stacy Bass, design: Angela Camarda, Lillian August Designs **page 164:** *both* Mark Lohman; *left* design: Barclay Butera Inc. **page 166:** Stacy Bass, design: Jennifer Drolet, Drolet Interiors **page 167:** *top left* Stacy Bass, design: Patricia Lynch Design; *top right* Eric Roth; *bottom* Ken Hayden/Red Cover/Photoshot **page 168:** Tony Giammarino/Giammarino & Dworkin **page 169:** *top* Eric Roth, design: Bev Rivkind; bottom Eric Roth, design: MJ Berries **page 170:** Mark Lohman **page 171:** Mark Samu, design: Donald Billinkoff AIA **page 172:** Eric Roth, design: susansargent.com **page 173:** Tony Giammarino/Giammarino & Dworkin, design: DialMyersDesign.com **page 174:** Eric Roth, design: susansargent.com **page 175:** *top* melabee m miller, design: Nancee Brown, ASID; *bottom* Eric Roth, design: MJ Berries **page 176:** Tria Giovan,

design: Amanda Nisbet **page 177:** courtesy of Thibaut Inc. **pages 178–179:** *both* courtesy of Thibaut Inc. **pages 180–181:** Tony Giammarino/Giammarino & Dworkin **page 182:** Bob Greenspan, stylist: Susan Andrews **page 183:** Mark Samu **pages 184–185:** *left* Bob Greenspan, stylist: Susan Andrews; *right* Eric Roth **page 186:** *both* Mark Lohman; *bottom* design: Janet Lohman Interior Design **pages 187–188:** *both* Mark Samu **page 189:** *top* courtesy of Malibu Lighting/Intermatic, Inc; *bottom* Susan Gilmore, design: Martha O'Hara Interiors, oharainteriors.com **page 190:** *both* Karyn R. Millet; *right* design: Bonesteel Trout Hall **pages 192–193:** Roy Inman, stylist: Susan Andrews **pages 194–195:** *top left* Mark Lohman, design: Cynthia Marks Interior Design; *bottom left* Karyn R. Millet; *right* Eric Roth, design: duffydesigngroup.com **page 196:** Bob Greenspan, stylist: Susan Andrews **page 197:** *top* Mark Samu; *bottom* Olson Photographic, LLC **pages 198–199:** Eric Roth **page 200:** Ken Hayden/Red Cover/Photoshot, architect: Rene Gonzales **page 201:** *top* Tony Giammarino/Giammarino & Dworkin, design: Tom Duke of Evolve; *bottom* melabee m miller, design: Joyce Krieg **pages 202–203:** *all* Karyn R. Millet; *middle left* design: Taylor Borsari **pages 204–205:** melabee m miller, design: Diane Romanowski **pages 206–207:** *both* Karyn R. Millet; *left* design: Joan Behnke & Associates **page 208:** courtesy of Robbins/Armstrong **page 209:** *top* courtesy of Armstrong; *bottom* courtesy of Hartco/Armstrong **pages 210–211:** courtesy of Hartco/Armstrong **page 212:** *top* courtesy of Armstrong; *bottom* courtesy of Mannington **page 213:** courtesy of Mannington **pages 214–215:** *all* courtesy of Teragren **page 216:** Mark Lohman **page 217:** *left* Karyn R. Millet, architect: The Warwick Group; *right* Mark Lohman **page 218:** courtesy of Mannington **page 219:** *top* courtesy of IVC; *bottom* courtesy of Armstrong **page 220:** *both* Mark Samu **page 221:** Eric Roth, design: johndd.com **pages 222–223:** *left & bottom middle* Karyn R. Millet, design: Michael Fullen, M2 Design; *top right* Olson Photographic, LLC, builder: VAS Construction **pages 224–225:** Olson Photographic, LLC **pages 226–227:** Karyn R. Millet **page 228:** *top* Mark Samu; *bottom* melabee m miller, design: Diane

Romanowski **page 229:** Karyn R. Millet **page 230:** Eric Roth, design: Griffin Interiors **page 231:** *top* Mark Samu; *bottom* Mark Lohman **pages 232–233:** *all* Mark Samu **page 234:** *top* melabee m miller, design: Marlene Wangenheim, ASID; *bottom* Olson Photographic, LLC, design: InnerSpace Electronics **page 235:** *both* Olson Photographic, LLC, design: InnerSpace Electronics **page 236:** *top* Anne Gummerson, builder: Taylor-Reed Builders; *bottom* Mark Samu **page 237:** *top* Olson Photographic, LLC; *bottom* Bob Greenspan, stylist: Susan Andrews **page 238:** *top* Mark Samu; *bottom* courtesy of Caesarstone **page 239:** *left* Eric Roth, design: Anamika Design; *right* Bob Greenspan, stylist: Susan Andrews **page 240:** Robin Stubbert/Red Cover/Photoshot **page 241:** Bob Greenspan, stylist: Susan Andrews **page 242:** *both* Mark Lohman; *left* design: Janet Lohman Interior Design; *right* design: Barclay Butera Inc. **page 243:** Susan Gilmore, design: David Heide Design, DHDStudio.com **pages 244–245:** Eric Roth, design: lauraglendesign.com **pages 246–247:** *all* Mark Lohman **pages 248–249:** *both* Mark Lohman, design: Janet Lohman Interior Design **pages 250–251:** *left* Eric Roth, design/builder: jwconstructioninc.com; *right* Karyn R. Millet **pages 252–253:** *top left* Stacy Bass, Mural by Mary Beall Mooney; *top right* Mark Lohman; *bottom right* Mark Lohman, design: Jan Dutcher **pages 254–255:** *both* Mark Lohman, design: Barclay Butera Inc. **pages 256–257:** *all* Bob Greenspan, stylist: Susan Andrews **page 258:** *both* courtesy of Merillat **page 259:** *left* courtesy of Merillat; *right* courtesy of Kraftmaid **page 260:** Eric Roth, design/architect: spacecraftarch.com **page 261:** *left* melabee m miller, design: Diane Romanowski; *right* davidduncanlivingston.com **page 262:** *left* Eric Roth, design: John DeBastiani; *right* Olson Photographic, LLC, design/builder: Design Build **page 263:** *left* Olson Photographic, LLC, design: Capitol designs; *top right* Eric Roth; *bottom right* Eric Roth, design: John DeBastiani **pages 264–265:** *all* Mark Samu **page 277:** Roy Inman, stylist: Susan Andrews **page 279:** Karyn R. Millet **page 280:** Eric Roth **page 283:** Eric Roth **page 284:** Stacy Bass, Mural by Mary Beall Mooney

Have a gardening, decorating, or home improvement project?
Look for these and other fine Creative Homeowner books
wherever books are sold

BEST SIGNATURE KITCHENS
A showcase of kitchens from top designers around the country.

Over 250 photographs.
240 pp.
8¼" × 10⅞"
$19.95 (US)
$23.95 (CAN)
BOOK #: CH279510

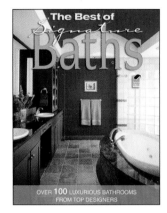

THE BEST OF SIGNATURE BATHS
Features luxurious and inspiring bathrooms from top designers.

Over 250 photographs.
240 pp.
8¼" × 10⅞"
$19.95 (US)
$21.95 (CAN)
BOOK #: CH279522

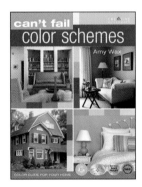

CAN'T FAIL COLOR SCHEMES
A take-it-with you visual guide to selecting color schemes and texture.

Over 300 photographs.
304 pp.
7" × 9¼"
$19.95 (US)
$21.95 (CAN)
BOOK #: CH279659

PAINT SAVES THE DAY
Provides inspiration and step-by-step instructions to transform your everyday items using paint.

Over 275 photographs.
208 pp.
8½" × 10⅞"
$19.95 (US)
$23.95 (CAN)
BOOK #: CH279575

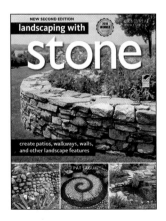

LANDSCAPING WITH STONE
Ideas for incorporating stone into the landscape.

Over 335 photographs.
224 pp.
8½" × 10⅞"
$19.95 (US)
$21.95 (CAN)
BOOK #: CH274179

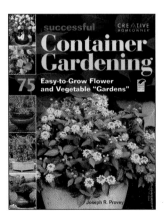

SUCCESSFUL CONTAINER GARDENING
Information to grow your own flower, fruit, and vegetable "gardens."

Over 240 photographs.
160 pp.
8½" × 10⅞"
$14.95 (US)
$17.95 (CAN)
BOOK #: CH274857

For more information and to order direct, go to **www.creativehomeowner.com**